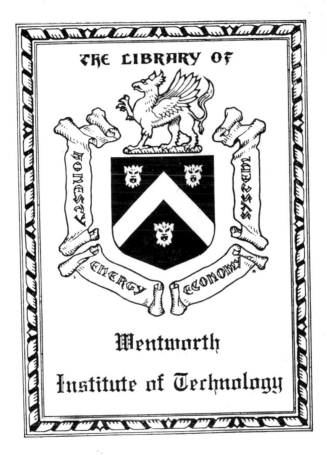

The Long Road North

The Long Road North

JOHN DAVIDSON

Doubleday & Company, Inc., Garden City, New York
1979

Part of this book first appeared in a slightly different form in an article entitled "The Long Road North" in *Texas Monthly*. Copyright © 1977 by Mediatex Communications Corporation.

331.62
D3

Library of Congress Cataloging in Publication Data

Davidson, John, 1947–
The long road north. — Garden City, N.Y. :
Doubleday, 1979.
1. Alien labor, Mexican—Texas. 2. Mexicans in
Texas. I. Title.
HD8081.M6D38   331.6′2′72073
ISBN: 0-385-14507-1
Library of Congress Catalog Card Number 78-22312

For Julie and Jinks

ACKNOWLEDGMENTS

A lot of people, some unwittingly, have helped with this book, but there are six who deserve special thanks:

Javier and Juan for taking me along

William Broyles at *Texas Monthly* for giving me cause to begin

Ken McCormick and Carolyn Blakemore at Doubleday & Company for making this book possible

And Suzanne Winckler for encouragement every step along the way

FOREWORD

IN THE DARK beneath the overpass, the men stood in loose lines on either side of the street. Above, a solitary truck passed on the expressway, disrupting the early quiet of downtown San Antonio. Some of the men stood alone; others stood talking in small groups. A white panel truck pulled in beneath the overpass, rolled to a stop, and the men rushed it. They swarmed the truck, trying to get the driver's attention. After a few moments' haggling, one of the men climbed in, the truck drove off, and the others drifted back to their places.

Across the street from me, I could make out two men in cowboy boots, hats, and jeans who appeared to be *rancheros* from Northern Mexico. There was also an older man in straw sombrero and sandals. They were standing among men who were either Mexican-Americans or urban Mexicans. When I started across the street, they floated down the sidewalk out of range.

The men had come to what economists call a shadow labor market. Each morning, the market forms beneath the expressway that divides the commercial center of San Antonio from the west-side slums. Mexicans without legal documents and Mexican-Americans on unemployment look for work. Small contractors who don't want to pay minimum wages or bother with Social Security look for workers. It is an old San Antonio institution that used to take place next to the farmers' market before it was renovated and turned over to tourists. I went there thinking I could stand in one of the lines, start a conversation with some of the men, and explain that I was a journalist who wanted to find out about wetbacks in San Antonio. Having a beard and wearing blue jeans, I hadn't worried about being mistaken for an immigration officer. But beneath the overpass, being Anglo was cause enough for suspicion.

A succession of panel trucks and pickups came. The lines dwindled as the sound of traffic above increased and the light grew. Each time I walked toward any of the men, they faded away before me. If I started across the street toward a group, they dispersed, acting as if they neither saw nor heard me. The only time I got near was when I would follow to the stopped vehicles where I could hear the bargaining over hours and wages.

When the traffic above reached its rush-hour roar and the

sun rose high enough to dispel the shadows, the pickups and panel trucks stopped coming. Among the men left waiting, there was a palpable air of disappointment as they realized the market was over and they hadn't been chosen. They stood for a while, then started drifting away. Disappointed myself, I picked out a young Mexican who was heading back into the slums and started after him. He walked slowly until he realized he was being followed, then increased his pace. I called to him in Spanish and walked faster, but he hurried on, refusing to look back. Grim yet amused at the idea of a chase, I lengthened my stride and was beginning to gain on him when I thought of how his heart must be beating. I stopped and watched him hurry down the street and disappear behind an old warehouse.

After a week in San Antonio looking for wetbacks, illegal aliens, undocumented workers, or whatever the appropriate euphemism happened to be, I had yet to talk to a Mexican without legal papers and was beginning to feel mildly frustrated. I had gone to San Antonio with the plan of making friends with wetbacks, establishing connections with their village in Mexico, and going there to make the trip north with the next group that came. Each day the plan seemed less realistic.

My main contact in San Antonio was a man I'll call Guillermo. I met him while working on another story about farmworkers in the Rio Grande Valley, where he told me that he himself had come to the United States as a wetback and was "King of the Wetbacks" in San Antonio. Graying, handsome, Guillermo worked as a union organizer and had a distinct rotten-tooth charm. Each morning when I went by his house to pick him up, he would appear unwashed and unshaven, drinking his first quart of beer. He had an anemic-looking, cowed young wife and several sickly children depressingly close in age.

Throughout the morning, Guillermo and I would make the rounds to the various minor politicians in the Mexican-American community. After long preludes of small talk and measured beer drinking, Guillermo would tell them what I wanted and they would say that of course they knew wetbacks, that the city was filled with wetbacks, but that they couldn't think of any right off. They would then give me the names of community workers—priests, nuns, social workers—and I'd take Guillermo home and spend the rest of the day looking up the new leads. The leads usually gave me the same response as the politicians, or, as one nun, Sister Somebody, did, would promise me I'd never find an illegal alien who would talk to an Anglo reporter. If the community workers had access, they guarded it closely; the politicians I began to think of as ducks floating indifferently on currents of hardship and poverty.

The absence of visible wetbacks combined with the official estimates that 40 per cent of San Antonio's unskilled labor force was undocumented fostered in me an uncomfortable sense of bewilderment. If the facts were accurate, where were the wetbacks? As with previous reporting excursions into subcultures that exist outside the law and are thought to represent an "underworld," I was struck by how well such groups of people blend into their environment and by how little appearances reveal. I was able to see only when I stopped worrying about the facts and stopped anticipating. Then it was possible to begin the leap from culture to culture, reality to reality.

The day before I went to the overpass, Guillermo had taken me to see Paco Cantu. Guillermo said that Paco worked with Tu Casa, an organization that aided illegal aliens in San Antonio, and that he would surely know wetbacks. When we arrived, Paco was working in the upholstery shop at the end of the wide gravel driveway next to his house. We could see him through the large, open garage doors tacking orange vinyl cloth to a chair. Short, square-faced, he gave the immediate impression of being intensely serious. He and Guillermo exchanged pleasantries in Spanish until Guillermo switched to English to introduce me. Paco, as a political act, it seemed, rejected English, and the three of us continued in Spanish. Guillermo explained what I wanted, and Paco turned his full suspicion upon me. Yes, he knew plenty of Mexicans without papers in San Antonio. Yes, the organization he worked with aided illegal aliens. But why should he trust me? Would I use names? Photographs? What did I think of the issues?

Simply asking the questions, considering the vulnerabilities, seemed to move him from suspicion to hostility, and I began to lose hope that he would help. In somewhat nervous Spanish, I agreed to no photographs, no names. They weren't necessary, nor did I want to expose anyone. Regarding issues, I would be glad to tell him what I thought, but my interest wasn't particularly political nor did I have a position to advance. I assumed that U.S. property owners and businessmen benefited from a supply of cheap labor, that many undocumented workers were treated badly, but I was unsure whether an open-border policy or an amnesty program would cause problems for competing Mexican-American workers. What I wanted, I explained, was to find one person whose story I could tell. I would tell it as honestly and as clearly as possible. It could speak for itself.

As if too annoyed to respond, Paco turned back to the seat he was covering, folded a seam of the vinyl, and began tacking it to the bottom. Seeing that I had nothing to lose, I went on and said what I really wanted to do was make the trip north the way Mexicans did. Paco and Guillermo looked at each other and pulled amused, disbelieving faces. "Ah," Guillermo imagined, "in el Río Grande, the boatmen would make a little horse out of you when they realized you were a gringo."

"Little horse?" I asked.

"In the river, they would climb on your neck the way children do, but they wouldn't let up and would ride you into the deep water. They would think you were either a spy or had money. Either way," he said with indifference.

"Unless he could pass for Salvadoreño," Paco qualified and looked at me. "They say a lot come from El Salvador and that they look like Anglos."

The talk turned to immigration politics and then to population politics, Guillermo and Paco projecting the high Mexican-American birth rate and the level of immigration to the time when Texas would have a Spanish-speaking majority. Paco finally turned back to me. "Come tomorrow afternoon," he said. "Perhaps someone will be here you can talk to."

When I went back the next afternoon, I felt fuzzy from having gone so early in the morning to the overpass. I parked my car in Paco's driveway and could see through the open garage doors to the shop where he and a young man stood talking in the shade. The young man was tall, rangy. He wore a white T-shirt, brown and white plaid polyester trousers, and platform shoes. Paco was leaning toward him intently as he spoke and barely bothered to nod as I approached. "¿Y el calor?" Paco was saying. What about the heat?

The young man shrugged his shoulders. "It's hot at work," he answered in Spanish. "What difference does it make?" Straight black hair fell below his collar, and the bristles of a sparse mustache and goatee suggested oriental TV villains. Sharp cheekbones, a long, slightly flattened nose, and acne scars added to the sinister impression.

"At work," Paco countered, "you don't step on snakes. It's going to be bad in the brush."

"There is no choice," the young man said. "My father is waiting." Then, as if to change the subject, he turned toward me and smiled. His eyes and straight white teeth diminished the villainous aspect. Paco introduced Javier and told him I was a journalist who wanted to ask a few questions. Javier looked at me and waited patiently as I floundered a moment, then said it was more than a few questions. I would need to spend some time with him.

Sympathetically, Javier said he would like to help but didn't have time. He was leaving for Mexico. My face regis-

tered enough disappointment and disbelief so that he
reached into his back pocket, pulled out a Western Union
telegram, and unfolded it as proof. It translated:

> COME TO NUEVO LAREDO. I AM WAITING IN THE ESTRELLA
> BLANCA BUS STATION. NO ECONOMIC RECOURSE. HURRY.
> YOUR FATHER, PEDRO MORELOS.

"A family problem," Javier explained gravely. "My father's come from Jalisco for help."

"Problem?"

"Someone is dying. Perhaps my mother, or," eyes widen-
ing, "perhaps she is already dead. This came two days ago,"
he pointed at the date on the telegram, "but I was working
out of town."

"And do you think your father is still waiting in the bus
station?" I asked.

"If he has no choice," Javier folded the telegram.

I told Javier I was sorry for his troubles, understood the
urgency, but wished I could talk to him for a few more minutes. I asked if he would walk with me to get a Coke at a
hamburger stand I had seen down the street. He hesitated a
moment, glanced at Paco, and said he would.

As we walked, Javier said he hadn't seen his family since
he left Mexico five years ago at the age of nineteen. His father farmed a small parcel of land—a remnant of hacienda
broken up and distributed among the peasants—but there
was nothing there for Javier to do. He had helped his father
until he was thirteen, when he left home to work on a poul-
try farm near Mexico City. That had been good work, he
had learned to give the chickens injections, had learned
about medicine, but the farm had finally closed and he was

left without work. He hadn't been able to find another job or get into a trade school because his father had taken him out of the second grade to help with the crops. Without at least a sixth-grade education, even though he had learned to read and write, there wasn't much for him to do but head north.

Javier said he wasn't nervous about talking to a journalist or afraid of being caught. At first, he had been scared and spent all of his time worrying and hiding, but had finally realized, through Paco's help, that he was doing nothing wrong, therefore shouldn't act as if he were guilty of a crime. All he did in Texas was work; he harmed no one. Was that wrong? I said I supposed it wasn't.

After we reached the hamburger stand, we bought Cokes and sat down on a curb in the shade of a hackberry tree. It was one of those first hot Texas days toward the end of May when you know it won't be cool again till fall. Not knowing how to begin, I bumbled and asked what it was like to be a wetback. We both smiled at the implausibility of summing up five years, and then he gazed thoughtfully at his hands. They looked to my eyes too old for his twenty-four years. The fingers were squeezed out of shape from heavy labor, and the skin was so thick it was like permanent work gloves. He absently rubbed a scar on the back of his left hand as if it might come off and said in his clear, quiet Spanish:

"Two years I worked on a roofing crew. I worked hard and the boss treated me like I was part of the family. His brother was my supervisor and we became *compadres*. I went to live in his house and shared a room with his son. His wife cooked and took care of my clothes like she did for all the rest. Every Saturday—we worked six days a week except when it rained—we got paid, and every Saturday the boss said he was holding my Saturday wages to save for me. After almost two years of work, I spilled hot tar on my hand." Javier held out his hand so I could see the scar. "I went to the boss and said I need to go to a doctor, but he told me to just put dirt on the burn. I went to the doctor anyway and missed a day of work. Not too long after that, I got a cold. It was a bad cold, and I had to stay in bed for a week. When I went back to work, my boss was angry. He told me, 'Javier, you're no good and you're lazy. Get out of here! Go back to Mexico where you belong!' None of what he said was true and it made me mad. I told him I was leaving but I wanted my Saturday wages. That's when he said, 'What wages?' He robbed me of almost two thousand dollars and there was nothing I could do. If I had complained too much, he would have turned me in to the Border Patrol."

I commiserated with Javier and said I wished he wasn't leaving, I would like to write his story.

"Perhaps when I come back," Javier allowed. "If I come back."

"You may not return?"

"Not if they need me there."

"How will you go?" I asked.

"*En las trocas.*"

"Trucks?"

"The ones that leave from near the market."

I didn't know what trucks he meant but asked, "And how will you come back from Mexico?"

"Swim the river and walk," he said, casually shaking the ice in the bottom of his paper cup.

"That's 150 miles."

"Perhaps someone will give me a ride."

Thinking how unlikely it was that he should agree, but knowing what a long time it might be till I had another chance, I asked Javier if I could make the trip with him.

"Do you mean take a car?" Javier asked.

"No, swim and walk. However you go." I didn't want to alter the trip, I explained, but would just follow along and do whatever Javier normally would. "I'll be your shadow," I proposed.

Javier looked at me doubtfully. "It's the wrong time of year. The grass is too high; too many snakes."

"It would make a good story," I countered.

Javier looked away, squinting as if to imagine the trip, and he began to smile. "If you made the trip," he nodded his head in approval, "then you would know what it's like. *Así podrías sacar el chiste:* That way you would get the joke."

And so it was agreed. We would leave for Mexico in two hours—long enough to make our separate arrangements and meet back at Paco's. I felt, walking back, the exhilaration and fear of any blind leap. I had no exact idea of where we were going, who I was going with, or even, more immediately, what "*las trocas*" were. But a door had briefly opened; I couldn't hesitate.

When we stopped in the upholstery shop to tell Paco the plan, he seemed surprised and doubtful. In his view, I was clearly excess baggage for Javier. "And how do you expect to cross him?" he asked Javier.

"He can swim." Javier looked at me for confirmation.

"But an Anglo," Paco shook his head. "What if the river is up and you have to get a boatman to smuggle you? He'll think this one is a spy. Or that he has drugs or money. You'll both be robbed and dropped in the river."

Javier looked at me and with perhaps less conviction than aversion for being told his business, said, "He can be from El Salvador. Salvadoreños look like gringos. And cross the river all the time."

"Hope it's dry," Paco counseled.

Before leaving, Javier instructed me to pack a change of clothes and a light jacket, and to wear boots to protect against snakes. Paco said he would arrange for one of the *trocas* to come by the shop and that I could leave my car in his driveway.

I drove to a travel agency to get a visa and then to the motel to pack and check out. Luckily, boots, jacket, and daypack remained in my car from an earlier trip. After I had put the few things in the daypack and stored the rest of my luggage in the trunk of the car, I sat down on the side of the bed in the motel room and called the magazine editor I was working with to say that I was leaving, that should anyone try to get in touch with me, I was simply "in Mexico." Paco was the only possible contact I could offer.

When I returned to the upholstery shop, Javier was standing in the driveway, a black portable radio in one hand, an orange and black flight bag in the other, and a black ball cap on his head. He was wearing high-heel cowboy boots, the same polyester plaid slacks, a brown permanent-press shirt, and a dark green velvet jacket trimmed with silver braid.

I parked the car as Paco directed and gave him the keys should he need to move it. Inspired by the transaction, Javier asked Paco if he would keep his identification. He put down his radio and bag, took out his wallet, and emptied it of the various cards he had acquired. "This way," Javier explained as he handed Paco the cards, "I don't lose them if we get caught."

"And *inmigración* won't know he's been here before," Paco added. "If they think it's his first time, they'll be less likely to investigate or press charges."

Paco offered to keep my identification, but I said I'd need it to get into Mexico. He suggested I mail it back once I was across and that we cut all the U.S. labels out of our clothes. Javier's cap, I noticed, had a caption stitched in red on a white patch that demanded, "What's your handle?" An angry red thumb stabbed at a waiting blank that remained resolutely nameless.

"Well," Javier announced, "here's *la troca*."

Expecting a vegetable or furniture truck, I looked to the end of the drive where a green van had stopped. We picked up our gear and shook hands with Paco, who followed us to the van telling us to take care and have luck.

"Six dollars each," the driver told us in Spanish. We paid, climbed in, and sat down next to a short, gray-haired Mexican woman. Her feet were resting on a wooden crate that forced her knees up and made the skirt of her purple knit dress slip down her thighs. Her hands she kept folded on a belly that strained the purple fabric, abetting the slippage until modesty required that she pull the hem tightly and momentarily over her rounded knees. She gave Javier a squinty, grandmother's smile through smudged glasses, and, but for a moment's hesitation, ignored me.

"I thought we were going in a truck," I whispered to Javier as the van pulled into the traffic.

"This is it," Javier answered. *Las trocas*, he explained, were like a taxi service that sent vans and cars nonstop between Laredo and San Antonio, and from San Antonio to Chicago. It was cheaper than the bus and you didn't have to go to the station. I had lived in Texas all my life, but had never heard of the service.

Next to me, the woman was asking Javier where he was going, if he was from Jalisco, how long he'd lived in San Antonio. "Ah well," she said when he told her five years, "then you have your papers all arranged."

Unimpeded by a response, the woman went on to tell Javier that she was on a shopping trip from Mexico City. She had traveled nonstop for twenty-four hours on a bus, had switched to a *troca* that morning in Laredo, and was now on her way back home. A man in Mexico, she said, paid her to come and buy things.

"And what did you buy?" Javier asked.

She glanced without curiosity at the crate beneath her feet. "Something to do with a machine," she said.

The driver stopped the van before a faded frame house and honked the horn. A middle-aged man looked through the screen door, then came out with a very old woman teetering at his side, a teen-age girl following behind with two suitcases. The driver got down and went up the sidewalk to help. Another woman, middle-aged, came out on the porch to wave good-bye. Watching from the van, it occurred to me that *trocas* were the same system as the *colectivos* I had used in Peru. It was as if a tendril of Latin American culture had uncurled and reached up into the United States.

The two men brought the woman to the open door. Through gogglelike spectacles so thick as to threaten toppling her forward, she peered into the van as though into an aquarium. Carefully, they lifted the woman onto the seat before ours. The granddaughter climbed in beside her; the driver slammed the door and took the suitcases to the back of the van. Slowly, the old woman's head swiveled so the magnified eyes could take in the van. She had, before we had traveled a block, engaged the woman from Mexico and was saying in a high, deaf voice that she was eighty-eight, tired of the doctors, and glad to be going home to Laredo where life was *calmado*.

The van wound through West San Antonio neighborhoods, stopping along the way to pick up passengers. One stop for two brassy Mexican women on their way home from an assault on the discount stores, and three stops for men, tired and empty-handed. As the van filled, I noticed that I was the only Anglo, that I had entered a conduit exclusively Spanish. The realization of how out of place I was made me expect comment or curiosity, but as each passenger got in and scanned the other faces, he or she would hesitate slightly at mine and then ignore me completely. I did not sense hostility, but began to have the strange feeling that I simply wasn't there. It was as if people not only don't

recognize what they don't know or understand, but also
don't recognize what is too far afield. It is a universal cul-
tural technique for obliterating what is alien.

The passengers were settling in, prodding identities, making themselves known for the trip. The old woman had
finished telling about her husband leaving her a widow
forty-three years earlier and had moved on to her cataract
operations. The granddaughter smiled as though she had
never heard it before.

Excluded, I began to think of all the last-minute things I
hadn't had time for. Iodine tablets for the water in Mexico,
bills at home that needed to be paid, my car abandoned
with a stranger—all of it trivia. Then, with a wince, I remembered that the following day was my father's seventieth
birthday. Family and friends were giving a large surprise
party. When I didn't show up, they would start calling, trying to find me. The thought that to them I would have essentially vanished worried me and gave me the strange feeling that I was in fact on the verge of disappearing.

Then I noticed Javier. Staring out the window, frowning,
his face registered intense concern. I thought of his father
and tried to imagine my own father stranded for two days in
a bus station waiting for me, tried to imagine going home
for the first time in five years to see whether my mother was
dead or dying. The attempt made me see how grave, how
much more serious Javier's concerns were than mine. By
right of gravity, it was Javier's trip, his story. I figured only
as an observer. And so, when the van stopped for the last
passenger, I no longer expected to be seen. I was willing to
travel as Javier's shadow.

Part I

A GATE IN the tin fence opened on a garden and green
shade. Inside, two women embraced on the gravel path
leading to a small frame house; then the woman in black
disengaged and came out to a van waiting in the street. The
driver took her brown valise and slid open the door to the
van. Trim, about sixty, the woman had short gray hair, was
wearing a suit and high heels, and made an impression of
being smartly dressed, if for an earlier time. As she hesitated
at the door for the driver to tell her where to sit in the
crowded van, the two brassy women in back nervously eyed
their packages that took up part of the seat. "*¡Ay, señor!*"
one of them started to complain bitterly to the driver.
"There isn't room for another passenger."

"¡Qué va!" the woman called back in a deep voice and laughed pleasantly. "Not go for want of a seat? When at this moment the groom is standing at the altar in Nuevo Laredo? And we've waited all these years? I'll sit on the floor before I leave him standing there."

The woman's good humor so completely undid the complaint that everyone in the van began to smile. The driver pulled a metal folding chair from beneath one of the seats and set it up in the aisle. The woman took her seat and announced that it was fine, then leaned to the window to wave good-bye to the older, peaceful-looking woman in the garden.

Through the thick lenses of her glasses, the eighty-eight-year-old woman peered at this new traveler. "This is your first marriage?" she asked.

The woman in black patted the old woman's hand. "It was just a joke. No one is waiting in Nuevo Laredo."

The old woman's face fell with disappointment. Everyone laughed at her gullibility and then again at their own. Javier was smiling as he watched the door close on the green garden.

After a stop for gas, the van headed toward the expressway, then south to Laredo. Beyond the city's asphalt fringe, the countryside retained the last green before the sun scorched the vaguely rolling hills to the static tan of summer. The afternoon heat subsided, shadows lengthened on the green pastures, voices rose in the van against the wind and the sound of tires on pavement.

Javier watched the scenery. Other than with roofing

crews, he seldom got out of the city. He had a car, a 1966 Pontiac, but there was neither time nor money for unnecessary trips. He would have enjoyed the drive, the vacation from work, if each time he started to relax he hadn't thought of his father waiting in a bus station and of his mother.

To distract himself, Javier got out his radio and turned it on. The initial squawk of static interrupted conversations and turned heads. The grandmotherly woman sitting by him smoothed the purple hem out on her knees and asked sweetly, "*¿Le gusta la música?*"

"*Las noticias,*" Javier answered. He wanted to hear the news and not music. He lowered the volume and raised the radio to his ear to try to tune in a station. After a moment's uninterrupted static, he sighed, snapped the radio off, and set it down on the floor between his feet.

Denied news, Javier turned to his own thoughts. He considered himself a serious person, didn't drink, smoked little, and was wary of romantic involvements that would burden him with a large family. This earnestness he attributed to a childhood accident and the subsequent influence of his mother's family. When he was four, Javier's mother left him in town with her sister, Josefina. Javier and his five-year-old sister were playing in the street when a car ran over Javier, breaking the shin bones in his left leg, pushing jagged bone through the skin. His mother took him to the doctors, bought medicines, and gave him special care. As the leg healed, a special bond formed between mother and son. Years later, the family traced not only this attachment but also almost everything distinctive about Javier to the accident. When he grew to be five feet, eleven inches tall, everyone agreed it was because of the accident and the medicine Javier was given. They also agreed when his sister died a year and a half after the accident that the cause was not the kidney failure doctors diagnosed, but fright occasioned by the bloody spectacle.

A more easily traced result of the accident, however, was that Javier came under the influence of his maternal aunt, Josefina. After the hospital, his mother took him to Josefina's house to convalesce, and, once he was past the initial trauma, left him there for several months of recuperation. Josefina was more than glad to have him with her. An anomaly among Mexican women her age, she had declined the offers of marriage that came her way and missed the chance of having her own children. It was not that Josefina disliked men; she simply refused to marry one who didn't have good sense and wouldn't work. She was confident that she could take care of herself and didn't want a man who would drag her down or move her to the country.

When she was a child, Josefina had been moved from the city to the *campo*. Don Pedro, her father, worked in a factory making concrete forms until standing in water most of the day, as the job required, gave him arthritis and he had to quit. Having no option, he took his family to the *campo* where he had grown up. Years later, Josefina described life there as a "catastrophe of indolence"; according to Don Pedro, it was *una bolsa de oscuridad* or a pocket of darkness. But somehow, Josefina kept her eyes on the light and, at the first opportunity, moved back to the city. She met an older man and woman of means who took an interest in her. The woman taught her to sew and encouraged her to buy a sewing machine. Borrowing the money, Josefina purchased a second-hand, pedal-driven Singer and moved into the one-room house her family had abandoned. It was a bold step for a young woman, and she worked all the harder. She made dresses, nothing fancy, house dresses to sell in the market, from early in the morning till late at night. In the first years, she said that she sewed her eyes blind. But she was success-ful. She paid for the machine, began to save money, slowly expanded and improved the house, and finally had a second-floor apartment built so that she would have rent income. She was the one member of her family who, by hard work, had made it out of the pocket of darkness.

In the time that Javier was with her, Josefina began a campaign of propaganda and example that would continue at every opportunity throughout Javier's youth. It distressed Josefina that Javier's mother and their other brothers and sisters were, in Josefina's mind, living like animals, raising children like "ignorant little donkeys." Josefina also knew that her brothers and sisters, rather than admiring her suc-cess, were critical and thought her selfish. Javier provided Josefina not only companionship, but also gave her a chance to remake herself and create an ally.

After Javier's mother reclaimed him for the *campo*, he tended to gravitate to his mother and grandfather. Don Pedro told stories about going as a young man to the United States, where he laid railroad tracks with the Chinese in California, picked beets, and worked for two years in a Spokane lumber camp. Don Pedro said it snowed most of the year in Washington and that no one ever bothered him until he went to Chicago, where there was a fight between the labor unions and the companies. But by then, he had been away for five years and was ready to come home. Javier's father had also gone to Arizona in the 1950s as part of a government-sponsored Bracero program, but he rarely mentioned it. When Javier thought that neither Don Pedro nor his father had ever worried about *inmigración*, he imagined that they had had a much easier time than he did.

Through the window, Javier saw the exit sign for Devine and began to pay closer attention to the countryside. What he saw from the car going south, he would most likely see on foot going north. Devine, Pearsall, Dilley, Cotulla—the string of small towns now invisible except for exit signs on the expressway—were part of the formula to return. At night, the red lights of their radio towers marked the last eighty miles to San Antonio.

Javier took a cigarette and matches from his shirt pocket. To the west, he could see the sun grow larger as it began its late-afternoon descent; at his side the woman had gone slack and rocked gently against him in her sleep, the hem of her dress slipping away from her knees. The van ran south through Dilley, on to Cotulla; the land became drier, flatter. Except where fields had been root plowed, there was less grass, more mesquite brush. North of Cotulla, Javier noticed the sign indicating Carrizo Springs to the west. He would have to walk to that road if he crossed the Rio Grande above Laredo. He watched until the next road sign flashed by: Laredo—sixty-eight miles.

Past Cotulla, the interstate dwindled into an older and

bumpier two-lane highway that roused Javier's neighbor long enough for her to tug at her hem before falling back to sleep. Abruptly, the terrain changed from pale green mesquite flats to rolling hills matted with dark brush. Javier sat up for a better look. He was surprised by the uniform and peaceful surface of brush that he saw from the van; it revealed nothing of the stony hills and the shoulder-high, fifty-mile barricade of thorns that he knew were there.

Orange, the sun touched the horizon, turning, as it sank, the green swells to black. Horizontal rays of light struck a windmill on a prominent rise and recalled Javier's uncle going to a similar windmill for a drink. Three of them, halfway to San Antonio, had stopped to work at a ranch for food. His uncle drank, sat down to rest against a mesquite, and jumped up shouting, "¡Ay, me pico la vibora! ¡Me pico la vibora!" The rattlesnake, wrapped low in the tree, had struck him in the back. They stripped his uncle's shirt away, cut deep slits around the two punctures left by the fangs, and, with the palms of their hands, gathered the skin and flesh of his uncle's back to wring it of blood and poison. The blood ran, but they could see the venom in his uncle's eyes. He would have died, Javier knew, if the rancher hadn't had an injection of antivenin at the ranch.

The sky faded and the vehicle ran south. From behind, a pale green Border Patrol car passed the van, leaving Javier in a wake of anxiety. The two-lane highway branched into a divided four, and Javier turned in his seat for a better look at the Border Patrol station across the median where a man in uniform inspected north-bound vehicles.

Neon lights blinked on in the early dusk along the motel strip extending out from Laredo; the van rolled on to the termination of the expressway, exited into the narrow streets of the old section of town, and crept toward the International Bridge. Javier sat with radio and flight bag balanced ready on his knees. The thought that his father was just across the river brought a wave of anticipation followed immediately by another of anxiety. Javier waited impatiently while the driver parked the van in the last block before the bridge, then came around to open the door.

"*¡Ay, por fin!*" the woman next to him sighed with relief.

"*Sí, por fin,*" Javier agreed. A deep breath, a tug on the bill to secure his cap, and he climbed down to the sidewalk into the stream of bodies flowing toward the bridge. Compelled by the flow, Javier followed the narrow sidewalk to the bridge where it widened for a barricade of turnstiles. Across the street, in the sickly glow of neon, he could see an opposing stream of bodies passing through U. S. Customs. He dropped a nickel into a turnstile slot, stepped through, and committed himself to the long walk back.

The pace of traffic slowed on the bridge. Midway, Javier paused at the railing to look down at the river. Between the brush-choked banks, the water looked deep. A breeze gusted downriver, rippling the dark surface. To the west, beneath clouds hanging low on the horizon, a pale lip of incandescence glowed a last moment before night set in.

Javier's pace quickened near the end of the bridge when ahead, in the first block of Nuevo Laredo, he saw a sign with a large white star and the words "Estrella Blanca." Beneath it, a green and white bus was waiting. Javier pushed through a second turnstile, dodged beneath the railing separating the walkway from the street, and cut through the cars stopped for Mexican Customs. A guard shouted, but Javier ignored him and started up Avenida Guerrero toward the white star. The sidewalk before the terminal was clogged with a pool of people funneling onto the bus, and the air was filled with the smell of diesel fumes and the impatient sound of the idling motor. Imagining his father just beyond the crowd, Javier squeezed through to the glass doors. Within were rows of green metal lawn chairs bolted to the floor. The chairs were empty, and there was no one in the room except two clerks who stood talking behind the ticket counter. Javier pushed open the doors separating the noise and fumes from the stale heat of the room and crossed to the counter. The clerks, elevated by their white shirts and black ties, glanced up but continued their conversation. Javier sat his radio on the counter, his flight bag on the floor, and waited. A neon tube buzzed overhead. The clerks discussed the merits of small cars until Javier reached out and touched the nearest clerk's sleeve with his fingertips.

"*Una pregunta, por favor,*" Javier began with elaborate courtesy. "My father, I'm looking for him."

The clerk gazed at Javier without expression and waited; his colleague turned his attention to papers on a clipboard.

"He said he would wait for me here." Outside, the diesel engine revved as the driver changed gears.

"Not here," the clerk said, picked up a stack of cardboard

tags, and tapped one edge against the counter. "You misunderstood. Try Transportes del Norte."

Javier began to turn away, momentarily convinced he'd made a mistake, until he remembered the telegram. "Wait," he said and dug in his pocket. "My father sent me this." Javier unfolded the sheet of yellow paper and spread it on the counter. "Estrella Blanca," he said and pointed at the line. "My father sent it two days ago."

The clerk peered at the telegram. "No one has been waiting here. After two days, I would have noticed. Try the other terminal around the corner." He began to count the cardboard tags.

Javier watched him a moment, then folded the telegram. "Around the corner?" he repeated and the man nodded.

Javier picked up his radio and bag, and, noticing the door to the men's room, walked in. When he came out, the clerks were talking. Outside, the bus had disappeared and the sidewalk was empty. He walked up the street and around the corner to look in the other bus station. His father wasn't there. Not knowing what else to do, he walked back to Estrella Blanca, where he stood on the curb for a while hoping his father would appear. Across the street, merchants framed by open shopfronts of gaudy souvenirs and curios stood talking and watching. The traffic from the bridge had peaked, and, other than a few stragglers, the street was quiet. Remembering that he hadn't eaten all day and noticing a restaurant next to the bus station, Javier went in and took a seat at the counter. It was a long room painted dark green where as many of the customers were there to drink as to eat. After ordering, Javier took out the telegram—proof that he hadn't been dreaming—and studied it for a key to his father's whereabouts.

The waiter brought his bowl of *caldo* and orange Fanta. Javier spooned out the broth and vegetables until at the bottom of the bowl an island of meat and bone remained, which he attacked with the aid of a rolled tortilla. He drank the soda and carefully wiped his mouth and fingers with a small triangle of translucent tissue from a plastic dispenser. Taking up the telegram again, he leaned back from the counter and lighted a cigarette. The waiter came to take his plate, Javier paid, and asked directions to the telegraph office.

Farther into town, Javier found the Edificio de Telecomunicaciones. The interior of the vault, through the glass doors, was dim except for a light glowing out of the last of a long line of telegraph windows. Javier knocked on the glass and waited until a head poked out of the lighted window. A moment later, a door at the end of the long room opened, and an old man in a porter's uniform made his way across the floor. When he approached, Javier held up the telegram for him to see. The old man opened the door on the chill room and led the way, footsteps echoing over the mysterious clicking, to the last lighted window. At the window, Javier sat his radio and bag on the floor and spread the telegram out on the counter. A young man with freckles came to the window and asked what he could do.

"My father sent this," Javier said and slid the telegram across. He watched until the young man finished reading. "I can't find him and thought you might remember him, that he might have come back."

The young man picked up the telegram, motioned toward the line of telegraph windows, and starting to explain the implausibility of remembering a particular customer, noticed Javier's dejection. He hesitated, peered at the telegram as if into the past, but finally shook his head. "But there's another operator here," he said. "Let's see if he remembers." He disappeared and returned with another young man who, though he didn't recall Javier's father, said he would remember the name and watch should he come back.

"Perhaps someone gave him money," the first man said. "Perhaps he's gone home."

"Perhaps so," Javier said wistfully.

Outside, merchants lowered metal awnings on the last lighted shopfronts; a light, south breeze blew in from the desert; pale stars defined darkness above. Crossing the plaza, Javier saw figures moving beneath the slightly swaying treetops that shade the plaza. The pale shapes, as he drew closer, emerged from the shadows as *campesinos*— white shirts, pants, straw hats—standing in small groups, talking quietly, grouping and regrouping, the tiretread soles of their *guaraches* flapping dryly on the pavement. Seeing the men, Javier realized that, if still in town, his father would be among them. He scanned the figures, and, as in a promenade, circled the plaza, watching closely for his father's face.

As the night went by, the men on the plaza lay down to sleep like cattle in a pasture. Indian women and children, down from the mountains to beg, slept beneath blankets spread on the sidewalk. Javier picked a park bench and stretched out with the flight bag beneath his head, ball cap pulled over his eyes, and the radio beneath his knees for safekeeping. His Anglo companion took a seat on an adjacent bench and watched as Javier drifted off. Unaccustomed to the idea of sleeping in public, the Anglo tried to doze sitting up until the late hour and his fatigue convinced him of the wisdom of lying down. He slept fitfully, hearing voices that passed in the night, stray cars. At dawn, his clothes were wet with dew, his body sore from the chill.

The morning Javier spent waiting in the bus station. At noon, he asked a clerk which bus he should take to León, the town closest to his family. The clerk sold him a ticket for the one o'clock *salida* for San Luis Potosí, where he would have to change bus lines. The *salida*, a departure connected with a Greyhound arrival from San Antonio, would be leaving from the Mexican Customs and Immigration compound.

Javier changed dollars for pesos, ate lunch, and checked the plaza one last time for his father. At twelve-forty he entered the cyclone fence to the compound and boarded the hot, dirty bus. More passengers got on, the driver collected tickets, and an immigration officer came on board to inspect passports. *"Soy Mexicano,"* Javier told the officer when he came to the last seat where Javier had settled.

"It doesn't matter," the officer said. "You still have to have a passport."

"But no one told me."

"Get your things and get off the bus." He turned and started up the aisle before Javier could respond.

Javier sat staring at the receding khaki back and then,

when he realized the passengers in front of him were looking, blushed with anger and shame. The official turned at
the front of the bus and signaled impatiently with his hand
for Javier to follow. Everyone in the bus watched with curiosity as Javier came up the aisle with his bag and radio.

At the bottom of the steps, the man, heavy and graying,
waited till Javier got down, then marched away toward the
immigration office with Javier in tow. Halfway in the long
line of idling buses, he stopped and faced Javier. "What do
you think?" he scolded. "That Mexicans can wander around
this country like animals? That you don't need papers,
identification?" He looked at Javier with exasperation.

Javier met his gaze, then looked down at the points of his
brown boots. "I didn't know," Javier said and looked up
again. "Give me a break."

The man's exasperation shifted to fatherly concern. "Now
I have to take you to the office. They'll investigate you and
fine you. Then you'll miss your bus." He stepped out of sight
between two of the waiting buses.

"But I have to go home," Javier followed. "My mother is
sick in Jalisco. If I gave you the money for the fine, couldn't
you take care of it?"

"I shouldn't," the man said and looked over his shoulder
to see whether anyone was watching him take the bribe.
"But it's a hundred pesos."

The bus ran south across chalky desert spotted with steel-
blue cactus, through a mountain gap in the first outcropping
of the Sierra Madre Oriental, and east along the eroded

spine of the Sierra Nacatas to Saltillo. In Saltillo, Javier bought a supper of hard rolls stuffed with spiced meat that he ate on the bus as it headed due south through pan after pan of flat desert to San Luis Potosí. As he ate, he watched the sun set, then slept.

At three in the morning, the desert air was cold when the bus arrived in San Luis. Javier walked into the terminal, saw that the ticket counters were closed and that beyond, in a dimly lit section, the floor was scattered with bodies. Picking a corner spot, he lay down to sleep.

The first bus left for León at six that morning. Javier figured that if it arrived by ten, he would have time to walk to the market and catch the local to San Francisco del Rincón. From there it was fifteen miles of dirt tracks to his father's *parcela*. If he missed the dilapidated bus that once a day ferried *campesinos* and their goods to the market in San Francisco, he could walk and still be home by night. The thought, after five years, built excitement beneath his fatigue and dread.

Javier got off the bus in León with the idea that he was back on home ground. The bus station, however, had changed, he had to ask directions to find the market, and the city looked different. He found the bus for San Francisco del Rincón, and, somewhat reassured by the familiar traffic and noise of the market, got on to wait. One of the first passengers on, he watched closely as the other passengers boarded in hopes of seeing a familiar face. Recognizing no one, he picked up a newspaper on the floor and glanced through the stories of disasters and deformities purveyed in the pages of *¡Alarma!* He read with particular interest a re-

port of smugglers robbing and beating Mexicans who tried
to cross the Rio Grande, and a story about a youth flattened
by a train. Below the caption, *"Joven Aplastado,"* a photo-
graph showed two legs emerging whole from beneath a
large metal wheel.

When the bus arrived in San Francisco, Javier again had
the uneasy feeling of arriving home and finding it unfamil-
iar. The village hadn't changed. Javier had simply forgotten
what it was like. The closer he got to home, the longer five
years seemed. The bus stopped in a side street near the
market where other buses loaded and unloaded. A man selling slices of papaya, the black seeds shining like larvae attached to yellow flesh, pointed out a broken rusty bus and
told Javier it would leave for the country in an hour. Javier
wandered up the street to the treeless plaza and the entrance to the market. The sand grinding beneath his boots,
the dust, and the eroding adobe walls suggested the town's
loose footing in the desert. At the market entrance he
thought of gifts for his family, and ducked under the tent
cloth stretched over the central aisle and into the gloom
lighted by the phosphorescence of turquoise and crimson
polyester shawls. Beyond the stacks of clothing, the earthen-
ware pots, tin buckets, the ripe fruit crawling with flies, and
the glass cases of warm, purple meat, he stopped at a
grocer's stand and selected a large brick of candied guava
for his mother. To it he added mangos, a plastic bag of lard,
a bag of soap, bananas, and a box of crackers. He instructed
the grocer to pack it into a paper bag, placed his radio on
top, and left the market. As he stepped from beneath the
tent cloth, the sun hit him and he felt a wave of fatigue. He

crossed the plaza to a cafe where he could get coffee before catching the bus.

Packed with *campesinos* and livestock, listing beneath the mountain of cargo heaped on top, the bus whined, rattled, and ground its way out into the basin of sand. Stoically, the peasants walking in the road stepped aside and accepted the cloud of dust. Beyond, the land looked dry and hopelessly unproductive; cactus was the only green in a tan landscape beneath a hot, unclouded sky.

Halfway, they came to the headquarters of the hacienda where, before land reform, Javier's grandparents and great-grandparents had worked and lived. After years without whitewash, the plaster had weathered away on the adobe chapel, the main house, and the servants' quarters, leaving the compound an unrelieved brown the same as the ground it was built on. Javier had never seen the hacienda painted but had heard his grandfather talk about the days when the land had been properly cultivated, when there had been money for wells and fertilizers.

The bus went on without stopping. Hedgerows of spindly green cactus lined the sandy road; tall trees of cactus stood gaunt. With a catch, Javier recognized an old friend walking beside the road. "¡Bartolo!" he shouted, leaning out the window to wave, but the man stared back blankly, then waved to the bus.

At the base of a slight sandy rise, Javier got down from the bus and followed a dirt path. Fine dust puffed up around his cowboy boots, and, on the familiar ground, he was aware of the strangeness of his clothes, the canvas bag, and the sack of presents. Like a nimbus, the dust rose around him, and he could feel the dryness in his nostrils and taste it in his mouth. A dog barked in front of his aunt's adobe hut, and naked children, gray with dust, gathered in the hard-packed yard. His aunt appeared in the open doorway, where she stood watching his approach. She was barefoot, wore a straw hat, and, like the children, was coated with dust. Javier stopped before her, lowered the canvas bag and sack of presents, and removed his baseball cap. *"Tía,"* he said and slightly ducked his head.

She took in his appearance, the stubbly beard and mustache and the hair falling to his collar, then blinked her eyes once to clear her vision. "Javier," she solemnly shook his hand. *"Dios te ha olvidado."* God has forgotten you.

"No tía," Javier stepped back and smiled.

She looked at him closely, opened and closed her eyes three times in hard succession, and nodded her head affirmatively. *"Te perdiste la inocencia."* You've lost your innocence.

"No tía."

She blinked again, then pulled the corners of her mouth down to show disbelief. "Perhaps you married." A smile revealed white teeth. "We knew you married when you stopped sending money."

"No tía," Javier laughed with embarrassment. "I was sick. Then I had debts to pay."

Another exaggerated look of disbelief.

"But *tía,"* Javier's voice expressed concern, "what has happened here?"

"Don Pedro. He was hitching the horses to the wagon. The horses bolted and dragged the wagon over him."

Javier's response was first the simple relief that his mother wasn't dead or dying, then regret. "And how is he?"

"Who knows? Your mother and father took him to the hospital, where perhaps he will die." She blinked rapidly in case of tears. "Not an easy thing for an old man."

"I had better go," Javier said and picked up his things. "My mother will want to see me."

"No one is there."

"No one?"

"Fernanda, the little girls. Your mother and father are at the hospital."

"Then I'll talk to Fernanda before I go to the hospital."

From the sandy path, Javier could see down the dry gully to his parents' adobe hut. Wood smoke drifted out of the cooking lean-to, a dry wind sighed in the mesquite trees along the gully, and isolated sounds of livestock floated in on the rural silence. After five years, it all appeared unchanged except for a slight rearrangement of broken tools and litter radiating out from the front doorway. Low barricades of dry mesquite branches corraled a pig, a goat, and a few hens in front of the house; a white dog quivering with blotches of pink mange barked timidly before slinking away. Alerted by the barking, a girl in a straw hat came out of the house. She was pretty, about sixteen years old, and had a bright red plastic poppy woven into the end of each of her braids. She looked uncertainly at the Anglo, then cut her eyes as if it might make him disappear.

"Fernanda?" Javier tried. She looked at Javier and smiled

shyly. "Are you my sister, Fernanda?" he said and lowered
his belongings.

Barefoot like her aunt, she stepped forward squarely in
her loose cotton skirt and shook his hand. Then, caught with
emotion, she looked away.

"*Un amigo*," Javier explained his companion, causing her
to nod her head in recognition.

A little girl in a soiled yellow dress stood in the doorway
to the lean-to, with tears from the wood smoke running
down her cheeks. "And who is this?" Javier asked and
walked over to the little girl.

"Your sister, Paula," Fernanda answered.

· "Ah, she's new." Javier tipped his cap back, kneeled before her, and shook her hand with gravity. Smiling, she
rubbed at the tears, rearranging the smudges of dirt on her
face. Behind her, Javier could see into the lean-to, the ashes
and burning sticks of wood on the ground, his mother's few
cooking utensils, the four buckets of dirty water that his
mother and sisters had to carry a mile each day from the
well where they lowered the buckets on a rope.

"How long will you stay?" Fernanda asked. "Mama has
waited so long."

"Long enough to go to the hospital," Javier said and
glanced into the one-room hut with its double bed and dirt
floor where he and his brothers and sisters had grown up.
"If I'm gone too long, I lose my job in San Antonio."

Remembering the improvements that he had imagined his
money from San Antonio had bought, he stood and looked
around. Next to the house and the barricade of mesquite, a
pig slept soundly in the dust. A kid goat, eyeing the last dry

foliage at the top of the barricade above the pig, stepped onto the pig's slowly heaving back to pull at the mesquite, while a chicken, its breast red as if already plucked to eat, scavenged the yard. Seeing no improvement, Javier shook his head with despair. "Nothing here has changed," he said sadly.

"No, nor will it ever," Fernanda said, as if the fact reassured her.

The attitude she expressed was so endemic to the *campo*, so inimical of change, that it caused Javier to snap with irritation. "What has happened to my money? How was it spent?"

"Papa bought pieces of tin for the roof. A team of oxen."

"But does no one work here?"

Her eyes squinted with anger, his sister faced him. "I wash clothes, cook, carry water, watch the animals. We work."

"But to change things," he said with impatience.

"It's for men to change things." She glanced through the corner of her eyes at the horizon of sand and sky.

"What about Father?" Javier continued.

"He works. When he doesn't drink."

"And Juan?"

"He's like his father."

Javier turned angrily away and saw Juan come floating along the sandy path on an old balloon-tire bicycle. Younger and smaller than Javier, he wore sky-blue pants and a paler blue shirt. His features were fine; his black hair was long and heavy. Cavalier, ignorant of what he was getting into, he stepped off the bike, letting it roll away on its own till it fell to the ground. He shook back his hair, pulled a large black comb from his hip pocket, and ran it through his hair before stepping forward to shake hands with Javier and his companion.

Javier looked closely at Juan. "What have you been doing?"

Juan pushed his lips out, almost as if to display the fine, unshaven hairs of adolescence that shadowed his upper lip and the line of his jaw. "Working," he said.

"Don't tell me that," Javier said sharply. "You've been sitting here in the dirt doing nothing."

Juan shook his hair back from his face.

"If you want to work, come with me. You might grow up."

Impassive, Juan blinked once, like a shiny black crow inwardly focused on not falling off its wire. Then he walked into the house and came out with his extra clothing packed into a cracker box tied with a string.

"I want you to know one thing," Fernanda stepped in front of Javier. "From the money you sent, I never had a dress, a piece of candy, nothing for myself."

Javier frowned, then picked up the bag from the market. "This is for you," he handed her the radio. "The rest of this, divide among the others. Money for a dress, I'll send from San Antonio," he said and picked up the flight bag.

"You're going now?" Fernanda asked, her bare feet planted in the sand.

"To the hospital," Javier said.

Neither of the brothers spoke as they walked the sandy road to town. The Anglo walked along behind, wondering that no one had asked who he was or why he was there. He realized, for the first time, that he might in fact go unnoticed.

After several miles an old pickup stopped to let them ride in back. When they got down in San Francisco del Rincón, Javier broke the silence. "Where are they? The hospital or Red Cross?"

"Who knows?" Juan said sullenly, taking out his comb and running it through his hair. "Possibly they took him to León."

"You don't know?" Javier asked. "You haven't even asked where he is?"

"How could I?" Juan put away the comb. "They haven't come back."

Obviously puzzled, Javier asked, "But when did they take him?"

"When it happened. Late yesterday afternoon."

Javier stood and stared at him for a moment, then pulled the telegram out of his pocket. "But what about this?" He shoved the paper. "What was my father doing in Nuevo Laredo five days ago?"

Juan read the telegram and handed it back. "Last week was the garbanzo harvest. He was drunk. He wanders now when he drinks."

In San Francisco del Rincón, neither the hospital nor the Red Cross had seen their grandfather. They went on to

León, but couldn't find him in the hospitals there. Javier decided the old man was well and back at home. It wasn't until they boarded the bus to Nuevo Laredo that Juan suggested the funeral homes.

Part II

THE NUEVO LAREDO-BOUND bus slowed to a halt on the last descent into the desert. "*¿Hay muertos?*" a passenger asked in the dark. "Are there dead?" Out the window to his left Javier could see the waiting headlights of a long line of cars. "*Es otro camión,*" a man commented. Javier couldn't see the wrecked bus and was too tired to stand up and look. He leaned his head back and closed his eyes. After a while, he sensed the bus moving into the line of white headlights, then a flashing red light, and finally darkness.

When Javier woke again, the bus was splashing slowly through water. A wake angled out until it lapped at the house fronts along the street, and stranded cars rocked gently as the bus proceeded into deeper water. "*Está hun-*

dido Nuevo Laredo," a voice in the dark softly exclaimed the obvious. Looking at the flooded streets, Javier thought of the river. If it was flooded, they couldn't swim. A smuggler would have to take them across. Too tired to worry about it, Javier leaned his head against the window and closed his eyes.

When the bus pulled into the Nuevo Laredo terminal it was 3 A.M. Javier shook Juan awake, the Anglo stood, and they gathered their belongings to get off. Downtown, the water had run off into the river, and the streets were deserted. Momentarily lost, the two brothers stood in the milky neon glow in front of the bus station until Javier asked the driver about a place to stay. Directed toward a cheap hotel, they started down the empty street, Juan carrying his cardboard box tied with a string and Javier his orange and black flight bag.

At the hotel, they got a small windowless room for four dollars. Without bothering to remove his clothes or black boots, Juan pulled the green bedspread back on the double bed and lay down on the spotted gray sheets. Javier took off his shirt and then his cowboy boots, which, to discourage scorpions, he propped upside down in the corner before switching off the bare bulb in the ceiling and lying down next to Juan.

They were all tired after the fifteen-hour bus ride from Jalisco and slept late the next morning. As they checked out, the woman at the desk showed them newspaper headlines that read *"CYCLONE!"* The storm killed three people and injured fifteen in Nuevo Laredo. Another twenty-eight people died when a bus crashed north of Monterrey. It had been the worst storm in years.

Outside it was hot, and the humidity rose off the damp ground and pavement. Javier and Juan walked directly to the bridge, then followed a chain-link fence west along the riverbank. At the railroad tracks that lead to the train bridge, Javier scrambled up the embankment, and Juan followed. On the other side, they dropped down into knee-high grass and mesquite and pushed through till hitting a trail. Garbage thrown from houses on the riverbank above was scattered along the trail, and there was the sweet smell of putrefaction. At the river's edge they could see the water, dense brown and pocked by whirling eddies, and farther out, rafts of river trash and the stately progression of floating tree trunks that marked the current's velocity.

"Can you swim?" Javier asked.

"Some," Juan answered.

"But not in this," Javier said and smiled. "You would get caught in the trash or a log would hit you. Then you would drown." He squatted on his heels to watch the river. "I wonder how many have drowned in this?"

Juan looked at him.

"No one knows what happens to the ones trying to cross. In the river, we're neither here nor there, so no one counts."

Juan shrugged indifferently and settled on his heels to watch the river. They turned in unison as a man came around a bend in the trail. His pant legs were rolled above the knee, and his bare feet stuck in an old pair of unlaced shoes. He was carrying his shirt in his hand. "Lots of water," Javier greeted him.

"Enough," the man agreed.

"How long will the river be up?"

"Who knows," the man answered as he passed. "A week. Maybe more."

They watched the man till he disappeared around the next bend, then turned back to the river. "What do you think?" Javier asked. "Will we make it or not?"

"*Pues, sí,*" Juan shrugged noncommittally.

"We'll see," Javier said and stood up.

Climbing out of the river bottom, Javier indicated what appeared to be an impenetrable thicket of mesquite. Grass rose a foot and a half to an intricate crisscross of mesquite limbs that formed a green wall. "The first fifty miles," he said, "it's like this. Only worse." He turned and climbed the bank to the railroad tracks.

In town, they waded through the jam of American tourists and Mexican vendors on the narrow sidewalks. Away from the bridge and past the market and curio shops, they found an inexpensive restaurant where each ordered carne guisada, tortillas, frijoles, and Pepsi-Cola. They ate slowly, using pieces of tortilla to tear the stewed meat into delicate shreds, which they rolled with beans and salsa into small tacos. When he finished, Javier cleaned his teeth with a napkin and got out his cigarettes.

From the restaurant, they walked to a small corner grocery store. Javier selected two plastic net shopping bags: one blue and green plaid, and the other orange and yellow. He asked the woman behind the counter for six cans of refried beans, six cans of large sardines, a small bottle of *salsa picante*, two loaves of Bimbo white bread, five packages of crackers, four packages of Parade cigarettes, several boxes of matches, and a bottle of rubbing alcohol. After paying the woman, Javier distributed the purchases between the two plastic bags, tied the strap of his canvas bag to the plastic handles of one shopping bag, and draped them both over his right shoulder like saddlebags. Juan transferred the shirt and pair of pants from his cardboard box into his shopping bag and they stepped back into the street.

At a hardware store, Javier bought a compass for himself and a white straw hat for Juan, which, on closer inspection, turned out to be plastic. So equipped, they retraced their steps down Avenida Guerrero toward the bridge, turned west, and in the early-afternoon sun, walked out past the railroad station, the cemetery, and into the slums of Nuevo Laredo.

On the low side of the streets, the soggy contents of houses were draped on fences and shrubs or stacked on any dry surface to catch the sun. Block after block, the houses became poorer until the town finally petered out with one last corner grocery. Squatting in the shade against the wall, a man watched them approach. "Hey!" he called when they got closer. "Where you going?"

"*Más allá*," Javier evaded. Farther on.

"Toward Carrizo?" The man stood to face them. Beneath his straw hat, he had yellow eyes and a three-day growth of beard. "A truck is coming that will take you."

"We'll see," Javier answered, and they walked into the store. Inside, he asked the *señora* for an empty half-gallon plastic milk bottle and bought himself and Juan a Pepsi. When they walked back out, a man was sitting in an old red pickup parked in the shade of the building next to the man with yellow eyes. The driver looked up from his friend and took in Juan and Javier with their boots, hats, and plastic net shopping bags. He made nothing of the Anglo. "I imagine you want to cross the river," he said.

"It's a possibility," Javier admitted.

"I can take you toward Carrizo where a man has a boat. Thirty dollars."

"Ten each?" Javier asked.

"That's right. Ten each."

Javier took out a ten and collected another from the Anglo. He handed the man the twenty dollars and put his bags in the back of the truck. "What about your friend?" the man asked.

Javier looked at Juan and shrugged. "He doesn't have any money."

"You could loan it to him," the man suggested.

"Not when I have barely enough to cross the river," Javier answered and started climbing in.

"Fifteen for both," the man offered.

"Leave him here," Javier said coldly and sat down in the back of the truck to indicate he was ready to leave. The driver looked down at his friend with yellow eyes, both shrugged, and he started the engine. As the truck drove away from the store, Juan and Javier looked at each other but made no sign. As they pulled on to the road, the driver glanced into the mirror and saw Juan standing forlornly with his shopping bag. He stepped on the clutch and the brake, leaned out the window, and shouted angrily, "All right. Get in!"

The truck ran west along the gravel road a mile south of and parallel to the river. Where the land was low and flat, standing water came up to the truck's axle and the flooded mesquite flats looked like swamps shimmering with heat, reflecting the blue sky with its stray white clouds. Speaking above the sound of crunching gravel and the partially submerged muffler, Javier touched Juan's arm and said, "We may have to walk all of tonight in water."

Impassive, Juan finished tearing a rind of thumbnail with his teeth. "We cross tonight?"

"At sunset. If we can get away from the river at night, the airplane won't see us."

"Airplane?"

"From *inmigración*. They patrol with the airplane and in Jeeps and trucks." Then, pointing at the submerged pasture, "Do you think you can sleep in water?"

"I'd rather walk in it."

"Walk enough, and you can sleep anywhere," Javier assured him.

The truck faltered twice before reaching dry land and going on toward Carrizo. After half an hour on the road, they approached a small cluster of shacks where the driver brought his pickup to a halt in the middle of the road. Letting the motor idle, he opened the door and stood on the running board. "Here there is a man with a boat," he said.

Javier looked at the shacks and back toward Nuevo Laredo. "No, *señor*, too close. Here *la inmigración* would catch us for sure. Farther on." The driver started to argue, but got back in the truck. Twenty minutes and two ephemeral swamps later, they came to a large white warehouse, closed and overgrown with weeds and sunflowers. On the far side of the building the driver stopped the truck in front of a solitary shack. "For ten dollars," he complained when he got out of the truck, "this is as far as I take you."

Javier and Juan climbed down with their belongings. An undernourished adolescent in a large cowboy hat and black jeans tucked into cowboy boots loped out from the shack and stopped before them. "You want to cross the river," he said, his pale eyes tracking independently across them. Not knowing which eye focused and which stared into space, Javier hesitated and the driver said, "Héctor, where's Rodrigo?"

"He's coming now. Any minute," the boy promised. He was so thin—a backbone inside a ragged white T-shirt—it appeared unlikely that he could propel the cowboy boots. "Three others are already waiting. We'll take them all today."

"Then I'll leave these two with you," the driver said and got back in his truck. As he drove away, Juan and Javier followed Héctor to the shack, which was circumscribed by a ring of trash as far as the arm could throw. Away from the road, the tin shack, its roof weighted down with worn-out tires, had been expanded by a makeshift awning covered with huisache branches and a lean-to kitchen. An old Formica-and-chrome kitchen table and chairs sat in the shade of the awning.

"If you have food you want to heat," Héctor offered.

"Not now," Javier thanked him.

"Perhaps you have a cigarette you can give me?"

Javier took out his pack, gave Héctor and Juan each a cigarette, and took one himself. Javier started to sit down at the table beneath the awning after they had lighted the cigarettes. "Not here," Héctor stopped him. "Sometimes the *federales* come; you had better hide in the bushes." He led them out of the radius of trash and into the mesquite, where three men sat at the edge of a clearing around a washed-out campfire. Two of the men had paper bags at their sides and the third a black plastic shaving kit. "They're going too," Héctor said by way of introduction, and the three men nodded. Javier and Juan dropped their bags in the ring of ashes and sat down on the ground in the long shadows of the mesquite trees. Héctor squatted down beside them to finish the cigarette he was smoking. "*Güero*," he said after studying the Anglo for a moment. "Why don't you just walk across the bridge?"

"*Pues, no tengo documentos*," the Anglo said and looked nervously at Javier.

"But you would only have to say you were American. If they even asked."

"But I don't speak English."

One of Héctor's two eyes focused on him. "Where are you from? Not Mexico."

"El Salvador. *Soy de allá*."

"Don't the people speak Spanish there?" He swayed on his haunches. "I hear an accent."

"Yes, but my family speak German. My parents came from Germany. That's the language I spoke first."

Héctor rocked slightly forward, dropped the cigarette, and stood. "Very soon and Rodrigo will be here," he assured them one last time and started back to the shack.

They watched Héctor leave, then Javier asked the men where they come from. "*Veracruz, donde no vale la vida,*" the round-faced man sitting in the middle answered for the three. "And you?"

"Jalisco," Javier echoed. "Where life has no value." Javier stretched out on the ground, put his canvas bag beneath his head, and pulled a weed to chew on. "How long have you been waiting here?"

"Since midday," the same man answered. "What time is it now?"

Javier looked at his wristwatch. "Four o'clock." To the west he could see cumulus clouds building as if for the sunset.

"Rodrigo is probably getting drunk somewhere," the man speculated. "The skinny one with the eyes said they took nine this morning."

"Nine," Javier repeated. "That's a good business."

"Yes, but it's not a regular harvest."

"It never is," Javier agreed. "You've been before?"

"Yes, but not the others," the man answered.

"Then you're the one who knows the way?"

"I know which way is north."

"That's good," Javier said and pulled the long stem of the weed through his teeth to shred it. "The first time I went, one of us had a compass. We walked for three days and came to a big river. At last we thought we were getting out of the brush. We spent most of a morning looking for a place to cross before we realized it was the Rio Grande."

"You walked in a circle," the man said.

"That's right," Javier smiled. "The one with the compass

didn't know how to read it. Like idiots, we almost crossed back into Mexico."

"But you made it."

"Barely," Javier sat up, stretched, and then propped up on one elbow. "Just barely."

"How many days did it take?"

"Eleven to San Antonio. We almost starved in the brush before we got to Carrizo and had to stop at a ranch and work for food. They gave us each two dollars for three days of cutting mesquite posts and said if we didn't leave they would call *la migra*."

"Be glad they didn't need more posts. You would have worked more days for the same amount of money."

"True," Javier said and sat up farther. Gazing toward the man, he had noticed that beneath the cuffs of his green polyester trousers hung a set of plaid polyester cuffs. The other two men also had double sets of cuffs hanging above their boots. "You're wearing two pairs of pants," Javier pointed out.

In unison the three men looked down at their cuffs and then up. "For the snakes," the man in the middle explained.

"They must be bad now."

"Perhaps the rain makes them crawl up in the trees to stay dry."

Javier studied the mesquite around them to imagine the outcome of crawling snakes. "That way they would strike us in the face or on the arms, rather than on our boots." Juan shifted uneasily, attracting Javier's attention. "Snakes scare you," Javier asked.

"Psssh," Juan exhaled disgust and turned away.

"The last time," the man in the middle went on, "we found a corpse. Snakebite, we decided."

"Many say they've seen bodies. Thank God, I never have."

"Not a pleasant thing," the man assured Javier.

One of the men who hadn't spoken got up and walked out into the brush. When he returned, he was carrying a milk container like Javier's except that it was partially caved in and dirty from months on the ground. He hit it against his leg to knock the dent out and the dirt off.

"Does it leak?" one of them asked.

The man held it to his mouth and blew till it was full and he could blow no more. "No leaks," he announced and sat back down. "Good," the man in the middle said. "We can cut a stick for a plug."

"Or make a knot of grass," Javier suggested.

Héctor reappeared to ask for another cigarette and to say that Rodrigo would be there any minute. Reminded that they had been waiting most of the afternoon, the man in the middle got up and said he thought they would walk farther up the river to see if anyone else had a boat. "No more boats," Héctor warned. "Rodrigo comes and you're not here, he won't wait for you. He'll be angry that you left." The man shrugged; they picked up their belongings and started for the road. Héctor followed behind, cajoling and threatening.

Javier watched them go, then lay back down, resting his head on the canvas bag. "If we cross by sunset," he said, "that's soon enough." He pulled the brim of his baseball cap over his eyes and drifted off to sleep.

It was dusk when they heard the pickup. There was honk-
ing, then shouting and drunken laughter. Confident it was
not *federales*, Javier and Juan picked up their bags and
walked out toward the road. In the half light, they could see
a blur of activity between the shack and an old truck. A
radio was snapped on to jar the evening quiet, children ran,
a flame jumped before an old woman in the lean-to kitchen,
and an old man staggered at the side of the truck. Héctor,
when he saw the two brothers, brought Rodrigo out to talk.
Powerfully built, dressed completely in black, Rodrigo
acted as surly as he looked. "You want to cross," he said and
hitched his pants tighter. Splayed, tusklike teeth sprouted
from his upper gum when he opened his mouth.

Yes, they wanted to cross, Javier answered politely.

"You can pay?" He looked them over as if it might be by
the pound.

Yes, Javier answered, they could pay. Without a word,
Rodrigo turned, walked to the shack, and dug in an ice
chest for a beer. He tilted the bottle back and drained it. A
woman in bulging red stretch pants came up and applied
herself to Rodrigo as if she in turn intended to drain him of
some vital force. Watching the galvanic weld, Héctor commented with approval. "Married last month."

Rodrigo disengaged, walked back, and hitched his pants.
"Tomorrow morning when it gets light, I'll take you across.
You can sleep tonight behind the warehouse."

Javier and Juan sat on the warehouse loading dock and
ate a can of refried beans. Above them they could hear bats
swoop, and before them the tops of six-foot-tall sunflowers
swayed at the edge of the dock. Juan coughed dryly on the

first wad of beans spread thick on a soda cracker. He
reached for the empty milk container and started to get up.
"Where are you going?" Javier asked.

"To ask for water."

"Don't ask them for anything. If they don't rob us we'll be
lucky." He spread a cracker with beans, shook some of the
red sauce on top, and handed it to Juan. "Let them forget
we're here."

After eating, they smoked a cigarette, then lay down on
the dock with their heads next to the wall. The night air was
cool, but the raw concrete beneath them was still warm
from the sun. At the edge of sleep, Javier heard someone on
the steps to the dock. Héctor came toward them carrying a
large bundle. "You want these?" he said and dropped a couple of blankets. They spread one blanket beneath them and
pulled the other over. "Tonight," Javier said happily as dirt
sprinkled onto them from the blanket, "we sleep like the
President."

Javier woke with the first gray light. He sat on the dock
and watched the shack. Above, a skim of clouds sped east
across the sky, a rooster crowed, but the shack remained silent while the protective dark slipped away. The sun was almost up when the door opened and a little girl ran out. She
pulled down her panties, squatted at the edge of the mesquite, then ran back to the shack. The sun rose and Javier
lay back down to wait. When he woke again, it was full day
and Rodrigo was in front of the shack washing his face in a
dishpan. Still dripping, he climbed the steps to the dock and
squatted down in a friendly way at the end of their blankets. "How much money do you have?" he asked.

"Twenty."

"Each?" he said and sucked his upper lip down over his teeth.

"Together," Javier answered.

Annoyed, Rodrigo ran a hand through his still-moist, wavy hair. "You think I can take you for that?"

"It's all we have," Javier replied.

"You'll have to give me more, a wristwatch or something of value," Rodrigo said and left the dock without waiting for a response.

Thirty minutes later, Héctor appeared and said they should follow him. Carrying their plastic shopping bags, Javier and Juan trotted behind him across the road and through a corn field toward the river. Overhead, the sun had broken through the morning haze. The damp ground was steaming. They came out of the field onto a road that twisted and turned toward the river. From behind, they heard horses and saw Rodrigo approaching in an old wagon hitched to two red nags. The old man and another man they hadn't seen before were chasing the wagon, and Rodrigo was beating the horses with a heavy knotted rope. The wagon, a wooden relic adapted with automobile tires, was too large for the horses, but bolting, eyes rolling, they caught up with Javier and Juan and forced them off the road. As it passed, they could see the boat—two automobile hoods welded together—bumping up and down in the wagonbed.

At the mouth of a ravine, the horses and wagon stood beneath a stand of large pecan trees. Héctor led the brothers down a path into the ravine. At the end, they could see

Rodrigo and the two men waiting on a small knoll above the river, the boat floating below in the water. As if barring the way, Rodrigo stood to face them. "How much can you pay me?" he started over.

"Twenty dollars," Javier repeated.

"That's not enough," Rodrigo said angrily. "I take *la raza* across; I help *la raza*. It's a good thing I do, but I must be paid. If caught, I go to prison and my family starves."

"It's all I have."

"What about your wristwatch? What kind is it?"

Javier looked at the dial. "Timex. It's old but I need it. I can't give it to you."

Rodrigo scowled at the Anglo. "What about you?"

"*Nada*," he said and showed empty hands.

Rodrigo turned his back on them. Héctor and the two men looked from Javier to Rodrigo and back to see who would give. The tension mounted until Javier repeated. "It's all I have."

"Then give me the money," Rodrigo relented.

They slid slowly down the bank on their heels to the boat, which had three crossboards for seats. Rodrigo stationed Juan and the Anglo in back, Javier in front, and climbed into the middle. Before telling Héctor to push them out, he studied the dense trees and brush on the opposite bank for movement. The mile of river they could see from bend to bend was clear, and the silence revealed no warning hum of a Border Patrol surveillance plane. Héctor shoved the boat into the swirling brown water, and Rodrigo dug in with oars made of plywood squares nailed to long sticks. With each heavy stroke, the two ends of the boat twisted at the welded seam, but by keeping within shelter of the bank, Rodrigo managed to row against the current without the two hoods splitting apart. The boat moved laboriously upstream until Rodrigo lifted the left oar and dug hard with the right to swing the boat into the current, then dug with both oars to propel them across the forty yards of river before it could sweep them too far downstream. Midway, a mat of trash caught and passed them, the individual sticks ticking against the tin hoods. Javier started to speak, but Rodrigo hushed him—a voice carries too far on water—and there was only the steady thunk of the oars in the notches cut into the side of the boat.

The prow of the boat hit bank at the edge of a canebrake and the passengers scrambled out into ankle-deep mud. Rodrigo handed up their bags and Juan shoved the boat back into the current. Staggering from the weight of the mud on their boots, they crashed through the cane and pushed their way up an overgrown ravine to a dry bank, where Javier sat down to slice thick wedges of mud off the bottom of his boots with a stick. He handed the stick to Juan and, breathing hard, whispered, "We have to get away from the river fast. No more noise." He stood, swung the plastic shopping bag counterbalanced by the weight of the canvas bag over his shoulder, and started north.

The heat of the river bottom was oppressive. Rather than shade, the trees and brush gave off humidity, and the lack of breeze was claustrophobic. Following behind, Juan could see Javier's dark brown shirt beginning to soak black and the empty water container bouncing loose in the plastic shopping bag.

Without slowing, they climbed a steep dirt bluff given to cave-in that marked an earlier meander of the Rio Grande and the outer edge of the river bottom. At the top, beyond a barbed-wire fence and dirt road that ran along the rim, they could see flat pastureland; below, a curving sweep of river and the lower Mexican bank. Javier stepped on a wire next to the fence post and jumped over. Juan followed and they sprinted across the road and through the open part of the pasture to the cover of a clump of mesquite trees. The ground was clear and they wove quickly through the mesquite until they came to another fence that separated the pasture from a field of corn. Again they jumped the fence and, crouched over, ran between two rows of corn to the next fence. The midday sun was fierce in the open field, and they were stung with sweat and panting for breath. The next pasture, where they spooked a small herd of cows, brought them uncomfortably near a farmhouse. They circled away through the mesquite, crossed another fence, and kept going until they heard the clear whine of pickup tires on hot asphalt. The tires thumped rhythmically across a bridge and whined away.

Breathing hard, Javier came to a halt beneath a large mesquite tree where he dropped his bags and sprawled on the ground. "*Carretera*," he rasped and nodded toward the highway when Juan dropped beside him; he was so dry, the cotton was edging out in gray flecks at the corner of his mouth. Juan sat fanning himself with his white hat and staring as Javier rummaged in his canvas bag and took out the compass to check directions. Sure they were going north, Javier climbed the mesquite as high as the limbs would take him and looked out toward the road. A car whined past, and when it disappeared, he dropped back to the ground. "We have to cross a bridge," he said and swung his bags over his shoulder.

Through the tops of the mesquite they could see a taller line of cottonwood and sycamore indicating a creek. Thick brush protected their approach to the bridge, and from its base they saw the water still running muddy from the storm. Javier dropped his bags at the foot of a concrete rampart and took the water bottle. "Stay here," he whispered when Juan started to follow him down to the creek. Juan sat down on the rampart and watched Javier crouch beyond a clump of willows to fill the container. From above, he could see a large black water moccasin uncoil in the willow and slide into the water.

"Did you see the snake?" Juan asked when Javier handed up the jug.

"I wish it was the last," he answered. His baseball cap was tilted back, his face was wet, and drops of water hung in the sparse hairs of his mustache and goatee. He watched with interest as Juan drank from the jug. Through the translucent plastic, the water showed brown. When Juan finished, Javier refilled the jug and put it in his shopping bag. "One at a time, we cross the bridge," he instructed. "Wait till I'm across and hidden, then you come. Listen for cars." He put his bags over his shoulders, and on all fours crawled up the rampart to the bridge. As he was about to haul himself over the concrete railing, they heard a diesel semitrailer, and he squatted down and waited for the truck to swoop thunderously past and drone on into the distance. Grinning at Juan, he pulled the baseball cap snug, climbed over the railing, and ran across the bridge. Juan could see him crouching and the plastic bag bouncing on his shoulder. In turn, he climbed the rampart, waited a moment, and ran across.

On the far side of the bridge, Javier was waiting out of sight at the bottom of the road's embankment. Juan waded down through knee-deep grass. They crossed the fence and started through a new pasture. The grass gave way to a hard, sandy crust shaded by mesquite trees, where they picked up the parallel tracks of a road. Javier looked back and stopped when he noticed Juan walking in one of the sandy tracks. "Step on the grass," he said. "You won't leave footprints." He turned and walked on.

The terrain began to change to hard rocky ground cut with shallow gullies and covered with low-lying scrub brush. Without the cover of mesquite trees, they were exposed to the hot sky and could see the land ahead begin to roll. Near what appeared to be a small abandoned feedlot, Javier cut away from the road through the thickest stand of brush until he came to an eroded ditch. At a clump of scrub oak that spanned the ditch, he dropped in and crawled into the shade. Juan crawled in behind, and, sitting on either side of the ditch, they passed the water jug back and forth. "What do you think?" Javier asked.

"It's not so bad," Juan answered.

"We haven't begun." Javier took a can of sardines out of the net shopping bag and cut it open with a pocketknife.

He put a piece of white bread on his palm, laid a large Mexican sardine on the bread, poured a little tomato sauce from the can, and rolled it up like a tortilla.

After they finished the sardines and half the loaf of bread, they drank more water and smoked a cigarette. But for the attention of blackflies, Javier felt he could go to sleep. He took the dark green velvet jacket out of his canvas bag, draped it over his head and ball cap, and leaned back against the wall of the ditch. "Rest!" he said from behind the dark veil and snuggled his body against the ground.

Juan covered the empty sardine can that was attracting flies and ants with sand and leaned back to try to sleep. He tilted his white hat over his eyes and crossed his arms, but a rock beneath his shoulder, then the blackflies, and finally Javier's heavy breathing distracted him. He crawled up on the edge of the ditch to stretch out flat, found that more comfortable, and dozed off. He woke to the sound of a four-wheel-drive vehicle winding through the brush. Not thinking they could have been seen in the ditch, but remembering his footsteps in the road, he cautiously slipped back into the ditch where Javier slept soundly. The winding sound came closer, slowed, then went on before coming to a halt. A pickup door slammed, a dog barked, and he heard a man's voice. In the ensuing silence, Juan sat in the ditch and stared down at the ground before him. Next to a dry leaf curled on the sand, movement focused his eyes on a scorpion scuttling his way. Meditatively, listening to the silence, Juan picked up a twig and stuck the end of it in the scorpion's path. The scorpion swung the stinger at the end of its long tail over its back at the twig, turned, and crabbed in the op-

posite direction. Again Juan blocked it with the twig, and
again the scorpion swung its stinger and turned. Each time
intercepted, the scorpion ran back and forth in the silence,
back and forth as the truck started and wound away into the
brush, back and forth across the sand until Juan crushed it
with the twig.

Javier breathed more deeply beneath his dark veil and
began to snore softly. With each draw of breath, the snoring
grew louder until the volume registered in the rise and fall
of the heavy velvet before his face. An abrupt snort, and he
pulled the jacket away and blinked at the light. "Was I snoring?" he asked Juan and smiled sheepishly.

"Loud," Juan answered.

"I dreamed I was snoring and the dream woke me up."

"It was no dream," Juan said.

Javier shook his head with sleepy amusement and then
noticed his wristwatch. "Four o'clock! Two hours I slept!"

"You're sleeping a lot," Juan commented.

"I wonder why," Javier said as he got up. And then with
irony, "I guess because it's my vacation."

Javier checked the compass, and they drank more water
before crawling out of the ditch. As the jug was low, Juan
suggested filling it at the feedlot, but Javier decided it
would be too dangerous. They cut through the brush and
climbed a fence where Javier found a cedar stave intended
as a support for barbed wire.

Beyond the fence, the land changed as if the abandoned
feedlot behind them were the last outpost and what followed were too inhospitable for agricultural enterprise. The
ground turned stony and the low rolling hills were covered

with an unbroken, shoulder-high thicket of brush. Parting the way with the cedar stick, Javier waded in, Juan following in his wake. Thorns dragged against each step, and stones, unseen beneath the foliage, staggered them. The brush rolled from swell to swell; the dark green troughs of blackbrush and ironwood were dappled with ashen ceniza and reefs of prickly pear, the crests were light green with fernlike guajillo. Slowly they waded until all they saw before and behind were the regular swells. Above, white blocks of cumulus marched east toward the Gulf, and a late-afternoon breeze rippled the surface of green.

Within the brush, the ground held the afternoon heat. Javier's shirt soaked black with perspiration; their accumulated scratches stung with sweat. They held the shopping bags before them like shields, but the nag of thorns was constant. The first variation of the landscape, a short caliche ledge, forced them down into a trough of false willow. The tops of the bushes above their heads filtered the light to an ammonia glow in which they saw a skeletal lattice of pale branches and a large ditch of stagnant water. The ground was sodden caliche, and white clay clung to their boots, miring each step. Slipping and staggering, goaded by moist suffocation, they forced their way through the thicket until the ditch dried and they were able to climb the opposite bank.

Crawling out, Juan stumbled and grabbed a branch of blackbrush, driving three of the long, straight thorns into his palm. He gave the branch a careful yank to pluck out the spines and then watched with interest as three drops of dark blood formed on his palm.

Thirsty, tired, red in the face, they pushed through the brush. At the top of a swell, they saw a small cloud of dust moving along the ground from east to west, and, as it came closer, heard the crunch of tires on gravel. The cloud passed about a mile before them and kept going until it disappeared.

For fifty feet on either side of the dirt road, the ground had been cleared so that the exposure and the distance they would have to run were increased. At the edge, they listened for traffic before dashing across the open space, crossing the fence, the road, another fence, and back into the brush. They kept going through the thinner secondary growth until Javier dropped his bags in a clearing on a slight rise and sat down in the evening shadow of a mesquite tree. Juan sank to the ground, Javier took out the jug, and they both drank. Due east on the horizon, near the road, they could see a windmill. Javier unbuttoned his soaked shirt and flapped it in the breeze to dry it. "This is going to smell," he grimaced. And then noticing that Juan was relatively dry, "Why don't you sweat?"

"Too thirsty," Juan answered.

Javier handed him the jug and watched him tilt it for another swallow. The muddy water had settled and a layer of silt approached the neck of the jug as Juan drank. When Juan lowered the jug, Javier asked him, "Now, what do you think? Do you think we'll make it?"

Juan handed him the jug and shrugged.

"At any rate, we've had luck," Javier said. "The airplane hasn't seen us." He took another swallow of the water and handed it to Juan. Juan studied the line of sediment, then drank slowly to avoid as much of it as possible. When he finished, the jug was essentially empty.

"Where do we get more water?" Juan asked.

"Windmills," Javier answered.

"That one?" Juan pointed to the one in view.

"It's too far out of the way. We'll come to others."

"Yes?"

"There are thirteen before Carrizo. With luck, it will be our lot to sleep next to one tonight." Javier took the compass out of his bag and checked directions. A light evening breeze had begun to blow, and the sun's rays were beginning to lose their intensity. "Let's walk," Javier said and got to his feet. "These are the good hours."

And on they went, one step after another, Javier always in front with his cedar stave and baseball cap, Juan just behind in his white plastic hat. Never complaining, never remarking the armadillos that crossed their path.

Two more roads and they came to a windmill. They opened the tap beneath the storage tank, let the water run clear, and Javier leaned down to drink. Salty. Juan drank as much as he could and they took turns holding their heads beneath the stream and running the cool water over their hands and arms. Javier took off his soaked brown shirt, rinsed it, and stored it in the net shopping bag. He put on a dark green shirt he'd been carrying in his canvas bag, they filled the jug with water, and, as there was another hour of light, checked the compass and moved on.

The sun neared the dark horizon, its long rays refracting pink on remnants of cloud, the sky turning an intense and late blue. In the last light, they crossed another dirt road.

Beyond, in the secondary growth of mesquite, Javier picked out a cleared spot that looked free of snakes. The sun touched the edge of the horizon and abruptly, as at sea, was gone.

The two brothers sat on the ground beneath the lilac sky eating refried beans on white bread. Juan had discovered that either the water jug or Javier's wet shirt had soaked the bread, but after considering spreading the slices out to dry overnight, they went ahead and ate the bread wet. Afterward, they stamped out places on the ground to sleep, Javier put on his velvet jacket, and they both lay down on the ground, their heads resting on the bags. In the dark, his back to Javier, Juan asked, "The life in San Antonio. Is it good?"

Javier thought a moment before answering. "It's work."

"But it's better than Mexico," Juan insisted.

"Harder than Mexico. More work. That's all it is—work."

"But you have a car."

"To go to work." Javier raised himself on one elbow to speak more clearly. "Everyone who goes thinks he'll make lots of money, that he'll have a chance. But you never have a chance."

"Then why are you going?"

"Who knows?" Javier said. "For the chance."

Javier lay back and didn't speak again. After a moment, his body jerked once and Juan could sense his falling asleep. In the night air, after the day's heat, it was suddenly cool, and Juan pushed his back to Javier's for warmth. The last thing Juan heard before dropping off was a high-pitched chorus of coyotes singing in the brush.

At twelve, they started walking again by the light of a quarter moon. The dark shiny leaves of the blackbrush and ironwood reflected the pale light, and the ceniza stood spectral. From the contour of the brush and the feel of the cedar stick, Javier was able to guide them through. When the ground was rough, he warned Juan. When the brush was eye-level thorny, he held it back with the stick. They watched the sky to set their course and stopped often to light matches and look at the compass. What relief there was from the heat was negated by the insecurity of each step.

At a thicket of prickly pear, they veered to the east to try to outflank it, but, after pushing through dense brush, were stopped by an arm of the thicket. They backtracked and forced their way to the west, but again found themselves outflanked. The prickly pear appeared to encircle them, as if like fish, they had swum into a trap. Within the thicket, the brush and the dark prevented their seeing where they had entered, and they were unable to gauge the depth of the prickly pear they would have to penetrate. Disoriented, Javier checked the compass and then sighted a narrow indentation to the north. He placed the end of his cedar stick against a branch of the obtruding cacti and pushed slowly until it broke with a vegetable crunch and fell out of the way. With the end of the cedar stick, he slowly and patiently punched a narrow hole through a four-foot-high wall of prickly pear, and on they went.

Coyotes sang in the night, the sky turned gray, they lay down to sleep again. By eight o'clock it was hot in the brush and again they were walking. By noon they had almost depleted the salty water just trying to keep their mouths wet. Their faces were a perpetual shade of red beneath their hats; their clothing was soaked with sweat; their eyes stung with perspiration. They stopped to rest beneath a mesquite and, too hot and too dry to want them, ate beans and soda crackers, which, due to their shortage of saliva, stuck to their teeth and gums.

They rested till two before starting again. The brush quivered with heat beneath the afternoon sun, and the sky was devoid of clouds. Though they had crossed two dirt roads, they hadn't come to another windmill, and began to think they had passed them in the night. From the sun and the sweat, Javier's left eye started to itch and turn red. Occasionally, when they stopped to wet their mouths—an act that only defined the thirst—Javier would look up at the blank sky and shake his head. *"No quiere nublarse."* It doesn't want to cloud up, he would say, and smile sadly as if it were a small favor that he was being needlessly denied.

One sip after another of the water which, toward the end, was mere provocation, and finally the jug was empty. Their lips burned from the sun and they became acutely aware of their thirst. Tongue, palate, lining of the mouth: It felt as if the tissues would swell and stick together. What wasn't the heat, a branch in the face, or the next footstep was beyond their attention. Twice they saw rattlesnakes—one coiled and one moving through the grass—and twice they ignored them.

Slowly, the Anglo began to fall behind. Heels blistered, left kneecap grinding, each step became an act of will, a taunt that he wouldn't make it. He watched Juan and Javier moving steadily ahead and wondered how they did it, how they kept putting one foot before the other. It was a simple proposition, but try as he might he couldn't move his legs any faster. When he had fallen thirty yards behind, Javier looked back and stopped. He stood patiently with Juan until the Anglo caught up, then started walking again. Again the Anglo fell behind, and again the brothers waited.

"*¿Qué pasa?*" Javier finally asked after the third wait. "Is something wrong?"

"My heels are blistered and my knee hurts."

A look of sympathy crossed Javier's red, perspiring face. "We'll walk more slowly."

"I don't know if I can make it. Each step hurts."

"You can make it," Javier promised. Then as reassurance, "One time, I stuck a thorn in my arm. Maybe the thorn was poison, maybe I got an infection. Whatever, my whole arm swelled up till I thought it might have to be amputated. But I kept walking. You can make it." He turned and started to walk.

The Anglo followed behind, thinking of Javier's swollen arm and wondering if his heels would become infected. Since the blisters had broken, he had chosen not to look. He tried to concentrate on something else and thought of how when running, it was possible to outdistance pain. Sports were the only experience he had to rely on. Looking ahead, he saw Javier and Juan's hats moving across the sea of brush beneath the hot sky and realized that for once it wasn't a game.

The brothers waited at the top of a rise. "There's a road below," Javier said when the Anglo caught up. "We'll rest on the other side." They went on and the Anglo followed. He hobbled across the dirt road as fast as he could, entered the thinned brush, and found Javier and Juan sitting in the shade of a mesquite. Just as he started to sit down, he heard the sound of a truck, its tires on the hard dirt road. They listened without comment till the truck was out of range. "Sit down and rest," Javier said after the truck was gone.

"I'm not going on."

Javier frowned and rocked forward from the waist in an affirmative gesture. "You can make it."

"If I had to, perhaps. But it isn't necessary."

"We can't leave you here," Javier objected.

"I'll walk back to the road. Now I'm only slowing you down."

"Out here, no one will help you."

"They will."

Javier shook his head sadly and started to argue.

"I'm sorry," the Anglo said, "but I've decided." He took out a pen and a piece of paper and wrote down a number. "If you get to a ranch or somewhere you can telephone, call and I'll come and get you. If not, call me as soon as you get to San Antonio."

Javier studied the slip of paper for a moment, then stuck it in his pocket.

"I'm sorry."

Javier shrugged. "If you can't go on."

Rather than relief, a feeling of emptiness set in at the road. Nor was there relief on finally getting a ride or getting home. The long-anticipated pleasures of a hot shower and clean sheets were undone by recurring visual flashes of Javier and Juan's hats moving across the brush beneath the hot sky. The first days were spent waiting by the telephone, fearing the insubstantiality of a number written on a slip of paper, regarding the expanding summer heat outside the air-conditioned apartment. After five days, Javier and Juan were assumed caught. After ten days, they were given up for lost. When, late at night, the telephone finally rang, there was silence at the other end as if a wrong number had been dialed. "Juan," Javier finally said.

"Javier! *¡Por fin!*"

"*¿Qué pasa?*" he said, his voice hollow with fatigue.

"What happened?"

"*Pues . . .*"

"Wait, I'll come there."

After the Anglo left, Javier and Juan sat in the shade of the mesquite until thirst overcame fatigue, then started walking. At five they came to a windmill. The water was salty, but they no longer cared. It freed their mouths and they took off their shirts to soak with water and sponge themselves. After they had slaked their thirst, they sat beneath the water tank to rest. "How far?" Juan asked.

Javier thought of how long they had walked before saying, "Tomorrow we come to a highway not far from Carrizo. From there, it's ninety miles to San Antonio."

"Ninety miles," Juan repeated.

"But who knows?" Javier said. "Perhaps someone will give us a ride."

They walked till sundown, ate, and slept. When the moon rose, they walked. At dawn they found a windmill, where they rested until the morning heat drove them on. Again the sky was cloudless; the heat, visible, audible. The brush trembled with the transmission of the sun's rays passing through, rebounding up from the ground and shimmering humidly above; an insect's buzzing climbed slowly, reaching higher and higher cycles of vibration yet hitting no limit.

During the night, Javier's eye had continued to itch, and with the renewed heat and sweat and rubbing, started to swell closed. By midmorning his eyelids had swollen into a puffed slit through which Juan could see bloodshot veins radiating out from the black iris. When they stopped at noon, the eye was sealed shut, they were low on water, and they discovered a new torment. Black lusterless flies, small and flat, clung to their pants legs and rode along peacefully until they came to a halt. Then, in a swarm, they attacked hands, faces, and necks, sending the two brothers into a slapping frenzy. Spurred by the flies, they moved on through the heat of the day.

After more than an hour without water, Javier and Juan saw a windmill on the horizon. Their relief, however, slowly turned to despair when, goal in view, they saw how tedious their progress was. In the afternoon heat growing to a crescendo, in their thirst and exhaustion, the windmill appeared to advance before them on the horizon.

The windmill, they found, was surrounded by a deerproof fence; large mesquite trees drooped around a dark pond of motionless water. The gate to the enclosure was padlocked, and within was a silent and ungrazed sanctuary of green. Javier climbed the gate, then Juan, and they jumped into the lush grass. Like shadows, black peccaries moved away from the far side of the pond. Midway to the windmill, knee-deep in grass, a deliberate and unequivocal rattle struck them like a current of electricity. Attached and rooted to the ground, statues in the glade, they listened to the warning fill the enclosure. Pulse hammering, breath shallow and constricted, neither could see the snake nor locate the sound. When it stopped, the silence was absolute and alarming.

They stood paralyzed until the silence waned. Javier lifted his cedar stick and tapped the ground before him. When there was no response, he continued to try the grass until sure there was no immediate danger of being struck. They moved forward two steps, prodded the grass, and continued the procedure until they reached the windmill. Still shaking, they washed their hands and faces, ran water over their heads, filled the jug, and left the enclosure.

Hastened by the thought of the road, goaded by their nearness to complete exhaustion, they plodded on. The heat broke at five and there was a light breeze, but by then each step forward was punishment, and Javier's eye was a swollen red patch. At the top of every crest, they thought they would see the highway. Each time they saw more brush.

The sun set and they stopped. Javier opened a can of sardines, which they ate with the last of the crackers, and sipping the last of the water, they sat in the dusk and smoked a cigarette. Juan stood up to kick out a spot to sleep and looked north. "¿*Qué es eso?*" he asked and pointed toward a red blinking light.

"What?" Javier asked with vague interest.

"There's a light."

Javier raised himself to his knees and sighted north through his good eye. "Carrizo! It must be the radio antenna at Carrizo. Come on," he said, getting to his feet, "we're almost there."

The red light winked at them as they walked, telling them how far it was and how slowly they moved. At the top of a hill, they could see a set of white headlights flash intermittently through the brush as a vehicle moved east to west. The next time they saw headlights they could hear the faint, mournful whine of a truck coming close and then receding in the night. The two brothers came to a pasture where the underbrush had been cleared and they walked quickly toward the road. At a fence, outside the possible sweep of headlights, they sat down on the ground to watch the pavement. "What do you think?" Javier asked. "If we ask for a ride, we might be in San Antonio tonight." He savored the idea. "Or *la inmigración* might catch us."

"And if we don't ask for a ride?" Juan said.

"Then we walk another seven days. More, if we have to work for food."

Juan looked straight ahead at the road and didn't answer.

"There are always risks," Javier decided and started for the fence.

The first car caught them in its headlights—Javier with his swollen eye and black baseball cap, Juan with his white hat —and speeded up. A pickup passed and then a large Oldsmobile sedan hit its brakes as soon as they appeared in the light and came sliding past them on the highway. They picked up their bags and ran toward the taillights. A man on the passenger side leaned out and shouted in a friendly voice, "*Vámonos a San Antonio.*"

Javier and Juan stopped running.

"*¿A donde van?*" the man called. "*¿Quieren un ride?*" Where you going? Want a ride?

Silence.

"*¿Van a San Antonio?*" he asked again.

Silence.

"*¿Son de México?*" he asked. Are you from Mexico?

"*Sí,*" Javier answered knowing that it was too late. "*Somos de México.*"

"*Bueno, vámonos a México,*" the man said. "*Somos de la inmigración.*"

"Pss," Juan hissed softly, taking a step toward the fence. Javier looked at him, shook his head, and dropped his bags on the pavement.

"That's right," a flashlight turned on them. "*¡No corres!*" Don't run. The Patrol Inspector climbed out of the car. He was a large man, made more imposing by khaki uniform, cowboy boots, and a pistol at his side. He held a long metal flashlight on the two brothers for a moment and then ducked his head back down to the car door. "Willie, I'm gonna check these ol' boys out for knives, real quick. Maybe you better check their tricky bags." Turning back to Juan and Javier, "*¿Traen cuchillos?*" They both shook their heads. "*¿No traen cuchillos? ¿Navajas? ¿Pistolas?*" They continued to shake their heads. "*¿No traen nada?*" he said in a teasing, disbelieving voice. *"Bueno, vamos a ver,"* he said and signaled to them to put their hands on the car to be searched. As he patted down Juan the other PI went through their bags with a flashlight, then stowed the bags in the trunk. "And what's this?" Mack feigned surprise when he felt the pocketknife in Javier's trousers. He pulled the knife out and held it up for Javier to see.

"Un cuchillo," Javier said.

"Come on, we're gonna be late," Willie called from behind the wheel.

"That's okay," Mack answered. "We're already two ahead of the game." Mack held the door for Juan and Javier, then got in front. "Want a knife?" he said and dropped the pocketknife on the seat next to Willie.

"Just what I need." Willie started the car. "Another cheap, Mexican pocketknife."

Mack sniffed the air appreciatively. "These ol' boys are smellin' pretty rich."

"And my ol' lady is gonna be plenty hacked if I bring her car back smellin' like wets."

"Two shouldn't mess it up too bad," Mack said. He turned in his seat to look at Juan and Javier. Javier was sitting by the window, and Juan next to him in the middle of the seat. *"Mala suerte,"* Mack smiled. Bad luck.

"Sí, mala suerte," Javier agreed.

Within two hours, the car obliterated what it had taken Javier and Juan three days to accomplish. On the edge of Laredo, they turned off the expressway and followed an east-west road to the Border Patrol station. Willie wheeled the car down the drive to the back parking lot full of PIs' cars and pickups and the pale green and white Border Patrol vehicles. Mack got Javier and Juan out of the car, Willie got their bags, and they crossed to the entrance of the main processing area. "Where'd you get them two?" a PI coming out the swinging double doors asked. "Aren't y'all just starting for the night?"

"Stopped up the road to take a leak," Mack explained. "Got back in the car and they'd crawled up to rest in the back seat."

"No shit," the PI said. "That's just about how many there are out there tonight. All this goddog talk about amnesty is bringin' 'em in."

"Makes us indispensable," Mack said sarcastically.

Inside, benches of downcast Mexicans sat waiting to be called before one of the bank of small desks where PIs sitting at old manual typewriters filled out the required forms. Willie left the two brothers on a bench next to an Indian woman holding a baby and followed Mack to check in. Most of the Mexicans looked exhausted, and none of them were talking.

Mack took a seat at one of the desks, rolled a form into the typewriter, and signaled for Javier to come forward. "*Apellido*," Mack said and looked up at Javier standing before the desk.

"Sánchez," Javier responded.

Using two fingers, Mack rapidly typed out the last name. "*Nombre*," he continued.

"Fernando," Javier answered. At the next desk, he noticed that Willie had called Juan forward.

"*Estado de residencia*," Mack asked.

"Guanajuato."

When Mack finished, he cranked the form out of the carriage, handed it and a pen to Javier, and showed him where to sign. "*¿Y el ojo?*" he asked, looking at the inflamed patch of skin around Javier's eye. "What happened?"

Javier put a finger to the swelling. "*No sé*," he said.

"You better get some medicine when they take you across the border," Mack said in Spanish. "You could lose that eye if you don't clear up the infection."

Javier thanked Mack, then followed him to a heavy wooden door that he unlocked, opening it on a rush of foul air from a small room. The room was lined with white tile, and like a steam room, had benches against the walls. Mexicans crowded the benches and lay on the floor; beyond, through an open door, Javier could see toilet stalls. "Good luck," Mack said as Javier stepped in, then closed and locked the door.

A few of the Mexicans looked up and nodded, but most were too miserable. Not seeing any space along the wall where he could sit, Javier picked a spot in the middle of the floor. He sat there, his spine and shoulders sagging forward with exhaustion, and waited for Juan. When Juan was brought in, they lay down together on the floor and slept.

In the morning, two PIs loaded them on a green-and-white bus to take them across the border. The bus crossed the International Bridge and passed through Mexican inspection before coming to a stop. Javier and Juan climbed

down with the others and then stood for a minute watching
the people stream back and forth across the bridge before
Javier turned and started into town. At the first pharmacy,
he stopped to buy eyewash and a can opener, spending all
but their last dollar. Then retracing their steps, they walked
back to the bridge, turned west, and walked to the railroad
trestle. They climbed the embankment, pushed through the
brush, and walked on until they came to a large oak next to
the river. Javier put the bags down, handed Juan the
eyewash, and lay down on his back. Juan studied the directions, then knelt beside him to drop the clear liquid into the
jellied space Javier held open between the puffy lids. Javier
blinked hard and then lay looking up at the wheeling
branches of the oak. "Here we rest," he said.

"Then what?" Juan asked.

"Start again."

For once not impassive, a flicker of surprise crossed Juan's
face. "How?" he asked.

"We'll think about it while we rest." Javier sat up to look at
the still swollen river. "But we'll make it." He looked at
Juan. "Do you know why?"

Juan shook his head.

"*La necesidad nos obliga,*" Javier said. Necessity obliges.

Part III

SLOWLY, THE BLACK TRAIN extended itself over the river as if elevated by its own rigidity rather than the steel truss of the bridge. Strident moans reverberated in the steel framework; metallic booms rang out from the couplings each time the locomotive halted. Juan watched the passage with interest from the shade of the riverbank. He and Javier were eating a lunch of their last package of crackers, which had been crushed, and their second-to-last can of beans. Sixteen hours of sleep had reduced their fatigue; the medicine had lessened the swelling of Javier's eye. From the cellophane package, Javier shook pieces of cracker onto the brown paste, then pressed in the white paving of crumbs to scoop it out on his fingertips.

"Where do you think it's going?" Juan asked. The locomotive touched the far bank, spanning the river with its black horizontal line.

"San Antonio," Javier said and handed over the beans. Then standing up to watch the train, he repeated softly, almost to himself, "San Antonio." He watched as the train slowly passed the sentry box at the end of the bridge until the caboose disappeared from sight.

The brothers lay waiting in the dark at the bottom of the embankment. On the tracks above, they could see a flashlight beam moving along the silent train, prying and worrying the couplings and the padlocked doors to boxcars. As it approached, they could hear the crunch of footsteps in the gravel of the railroad bed. The light entered and investigated the interior of an empty boxcar, its doors slid back to frame night sky within the dense silhouette. Satisfied, it moved on.

"Across the bridge," Juan whispered, "don't they check?"

"Maybe tonight they're lazy." Javier raised up on his knees and watched the flashlight move up the tracks. Satisfied it was out of range, he stood and picked up his bags, signaled to Juan, and started up the embankment. Stepping on the crossties, they moved quietly along the tracks to the open boxcar. A trapezoid of pale light fell across its floor, leaving either end of the car in pitch darkness. *Esperame aquí,* Javier whispered, sat his bags in the car, and boosted himself up. He disappeared into one end of the darkness, his footsteps echoing woodenly in the car.

"*Nada*," he reported, reappearing in the light. "There's nothing to hide behind." He disappeared into the other end, and this time Juan could hear him pause, then move something heavy. "Come here," Javier hissed from the darkness. "Bring our things!" Juan jumped up into the boxcar, picked up the bags, and moved into the darkness. A hand gripped his arm and Javier whispered, "There's a large piece of plywood. We can press ourselves against the back wall and lean it in front of us. But be careful; there are nails."

They positioned the piece of plywood before the wall, stepped behind it, and tilting it toward them, eased themselves to the floor. Settled, legs crossed tightly, they reached out and pulled their bags in on top. "*Está bien*," Javier remarked. "We'll look like the wall."

Within minutes, their legs began to fall asleep; a prickling sensation rose from their calves, followed by a dull ache. They made all minor adjustments, kneaded their legs, but the ache persisted. "*Ay, no lo soporto más*," Javier finally gave in, getting lamely to his feet. "If we stand, it will look almost as good."

They waited behind the board, listening to train whistles blow, wondering if the silent train they had boarded would cross that night. Down the tracks, a man whistled two long notes. Up the tracks, a man whistled back. "*La guardia*," Javier said softly. They pressed closer to the wall, drew the board to them, and listened, as, at intervals, the whistles closed. Footsteps sounded in the gravel beside the boxcar, a beam of light darted through, and in the distance, a metal collision resounded that rocked life through the train. The motion subsided and the train fell inert. Outside, the guard whistled. After a moment, there was another booming report of a car rolling into, coupling with the end of the train, followed by a shock wave of slow motion. From the opposite direction they heard the locomotive; its whistle sounded, the wheels of the car turned a revolution forward. Brakes squealed, then another turn forward. With each revolution, their anxiety lessened; each time wheels clicked at a rail juncture, hope mounted.

The train crept toward the bridge. Starting and stopping, it proceeded into the metal truss. The low reverberation of rails beneath the boxcar became an empty ringing whine. The brothers pressed closer to the wall and drew the board in. The whine continued, then dropped to a lower pitch when they left the bridge. Brakes squealed, and the train came to a halt. The brothers stood tense, listening to the waiting pulse of the train. Footsteps approached, there was a scrabbling at the boxcar door, and an uncertain voice called out as a flashlight came on, "¡Levantense las manos! Traigo pistola." Hands up! I have a pistol.

Juan and Javier raised their hands slowly above the plywood and stepped out, letting the board fall back against the wall. Before them, a small man stood holding a pistol and a flashlight. They could tell from the light that his hand quavered, as did his voice. "¡Bajanse!" he ordered and motioned them to the door.

They jumped from the car into the sentry-box spotlight and, hands up, turned to face him. Gray-haired, a clerk, the man fumbled with flashlight and pistol, crawling awkwardly down to the ground.

"Oiga, señor," Javier started, thinking of their bags behind the plywood, but the little man cut him off.

"¡No habla!" he snapped nervously, righting himself on the ground. He signaled to the locomotive with his flashlight and waved Juan and Javier toward the sentry box. From the doorway, he held the pistol on them while telephoning the Border Patrol. Car after car, the train clicked by until the caboose passed, leaving the night in silence.

At the Border Patrol station, Mack recognized Javier and Juan when they were brought in. *"Otra vez,"* he said to the brothers as he walked over. Then to the PI who brought them in, "Willie and I caught these two night before last. Be sure and get a file started on them. I'll pull the forms we've already got." Assuming a grave tone of voice in Spanish, he turned back to the two brothers. "You boys know what *la tuna* is? You've heard of the penitentiary in El Paso. We catch you one more time, that's where you go. Third time's the charm. Understand?" They both nodded. In a kinder tone of voice, "How about the eye?" he asked Javier. "You get some medicine?"

Javier nodded yes again and patted the small plastic bottle in his pants pocket.

The next morning, the green-and-white bus took them into Laredo and across the bridge. Empty-handed, they stood on the sidewalk watching the others disperse and the bus leave. "Now what?" Juan spit on the curb and looked up at Javier. Javier looked at him, then turned to the west and started walking.

Beneath the oak, Javier smoothed out a patch of ground and drew a wavy line with a twig. "This is the river," he said to himself. "Laredo," he drew an X on the line. "Here we can't cross. The water's too deep and they already know us." He drew another X several inches to the left on the wavy line. "Piedras Negras. Perhaps the water isn't deep; there they don't know us."

Juan frowned at the drawing and pulled a fingernail with his teeth. "How do we get to Piedras Negras?" he asked.

Javier drew another X several inches below the river. "Monterrey," he said, then drew a long line down from Laredo and a line up from Monterrey to Piedras Negras, forming an irregular V in the dirt. "We go by train."

Juan looked at the map, spit an invisible particle of fingernail off the tip of his tongue. "We have to go all the way back to Monterrey?" he asked. "Can't we go," he scratched a line between Laredo and Piedras Negras just below the river, "like this?"

"No road," Javier said. "No tracks."

"And food?"

"We have a dollar. After that, who knows?" He dusted out the drawing. "Perhaps we'll go starving."

The rails reflected the hot noon sun; the ties simmered with creosote. Javier and Juan walked south from the bridge till they came to the freight yard where signs warned that the area was off limits. Ignoring the warning, they continued on between two stationary trains, then climbed up on a coupling between boxcars to move closer to the loading

docks. Below, the massive wheels of the train formed an ir-
revocable conjunction with the steel rails. As they jumped
down from the coupling, they heard the blast of a locomotive and looked up to see it, its headlight paled by day, bearing down upon them. Trapped against the boxcars, they
watched wheel after wheel roll hypnotically by, and felt the
tilt of equilibrium, the gravitational pull of the rushing mass.
When the last car had passed, they started again. A man in
uniform shouted and started walking toward them. Rattled,
they backtracked out of the yard and circled around the
warehouses.

To the south, they stopped at a frame shack that backed
up to the tracks. A little girl clad in panties played beyond a
picket fence nailed together with random pieces of board.
She stared at Javier and Juan approaching, then ran for the
house. "*Señora*," Javier called out and knocked politely on
one of the boards in the gate. The yard within was hard-
packed; a tire, perhaps intended as a flower bed, emerged
from the ground like a relic in an archaeological dig. "*Una
pregunta, por favor*," Javier called to the woman who appeared in the doorway. Wiping her hands, she came out a
ways into the yard, the little girl trailing. "The trains," Javier signaled to the tracks. "When do they go to Monterrey?"

"All of them go," she said. The little girl, holding onto her
mother's dress, smiled at Juan, her teeth like the dissolved
remnants of licorice-filled mints.

"Ah, they all go," Javier repeated. "Then when does the
next one go?"

The woman looked in the direction of the freight yard. "This afternoon. Later this afternoon."

Javier thanked the woman, and they walked farther down the dirt road. At a shady spot where a huisache tree hung over a wire fence, Javier dropped to the ground. Juan sat down, leaned his back against the wire, and watched while Javier doctored his eye.

"Hungry?" Javier asked, blinking.

"Enough."

"We ate this time yesterday. By now, we're empty." He looked down at his stomach and poked it with a forefinger as if the difference might show. "Maybe we should eat."

"Eat what?" Juan asked.

"We have the dollar."

Juan bit at a fingernail and shrugged. Without speaking, Javier got to his feet and walked down the street. When he returned, he said, "I told the woman she could have the dollar if she would feed us. The food will be ready soon."

They waited in the shade until the woman came to the gate to call them. In her kitchen, she had put two plates of beans and two glasses of red Kool-Aid on her oilcloth-covered table. She stood at the stove while they ate, warming tortillas by dropping them onto the gas burner, then pinching them off with her fingers and dropping them on their plates. Javier and Juan ate their fill, gave the woman the dollar, and went back out to the huisache tree.

Late in the afternoon, they moved to a tree near the tracks. Heat waves still rose above the rails embedded in the oil-stained gravel; massive couplings resounded in the freight yard. The sun moved to the west as the day ebbed slowly away.

Just as they began to wonder if the woman had been right about a train leaving, a small electric pump car came out of the parallel strands, stopping twice while the driver got down at switching stations. Then, backing up, the pump car returned to the yard where it had come from, and minutes later they heard the blast of the locomotive and saw the signal lights on the track flash green. Two more sharp blasts, and the black-and-yellow face of the locomotive appeared, barely moving, slowly overcoming the train's inertia. At the flashing green light, the train perceptibly began to build momentum.

Javier signaled to Juan and they trotted down into the ditch and climbed the embankment to the railbed. Closed boxcar after closed boxcar rolled past, until Javier, over the noise of the train, shouted, "We want a flatbed or an open wagon. Someplace to sit." As they waited, the boxcars continued, and the train gained momentum. From their perspective, they could see neither what was coming on the track nor how much of the train was left. "Follow me!" Javier finally shouted to Juan.

Focusing on the narrow metal ladder that went up the side of an approaching boxcar, Javier began to run along beside the train, let the boxcar overtake him, and, as the ladder came even, reached up to a rung and swung his feet off the ground. To make room, he climbed quickly to the top of the ladder, where he could see up the tracks to a fast-approaching metal signal standard, and below, Juan running hard to catch the ladder. As Javier watched the impending collision, Juan came even, reached, and pulled himself on just before the metal standard whizzed past.

On top of the boxcar, they crawled out on the slanting roof to the narrow, slightly indented walkway that ran from end to end. A departing horn blast and the train picked up speed. From their perch, Javier and Juan watched the shacks, the trash, the waving children, the edges of Laredo fall behind. The boxcar, entering the desert, began to sway jerkily from side to side, threatening to throw them, forcing them to lie flat on the walkway. Head to head, they lay on their backs staring into the dome of blue.

"*La luna,*" Juan said, surprised to see the gibbous shape dimmed flat by daylight. Without the backdrop of darkness, it had no depth.

"It's come out to fill itself," Javier remarked. To the west, he could see the sun trailed by a cirrous tendril approach the horizon. It skimmed above the horizon, touched, dragged, and sank from sight, leaving a whirlpool of cirrus to mark the spot.

Cautiously Juan asked, "Are you still angry?"

"Angry?"

"Because of Father."

"No," Javier said, watching the darkness fall behind the moon. "It was something that happened."

"Grandfather," Juan said after a moment. "I wonder if he's dead."

"I don't think so," Javier said.

By moonlight, the desert became ghostly, the dry breeze chill. Twice the train stopped and twice the brothers slept.

While it moved, they clung to consciousness for fear the recurrent shudders would throw them off. The train slowly climbed the first outcroppings of the Sierra Madres; overhead, the moon stepped off the night.

When the moon began to sink in the west, the electric glow of Monterrey came into view to the south. They watched as the city lights slowly focused beneath the glowing lid of smog. Factories, houses, silent streets clicked past; the train slowed for a switching station, rolled slowly onto a siding, and with a final screeching of brakes came to a halt between two other trains in the freight yard. Javier stood and looked in either direction at row after row of boxcars. A final jerk of the train, and, to the front, Javier could see the untethered locomotive move lightly away. "*Vámonos,*" he said to Juan and started down the ladder.

They hesitated a moment between the trains until a swinging flashlight rounded the caboose and began to move toward them. Javier hoisted himself onto the coupling to the adjacent boxcars, jumped down, and went onto the next train. Listening to the giant domesticities of the trains, climbing from coupling to coupling, they worked their way across the freight yard until they came to a series of vacant tracks where they saw three triangular-shaped silhouettes standing at the end of a boxcar. The taller figure appeared to wear a crown and was flanked by the two smaller. Together, the three suggested the triangular symmetry of saints on a cathedral altar. Cigarettes glowed before their faces, and, as Javier drew closer, he saw that the three men were wrapped in badly soiled pink blankets, and that the one in the center wore a blue bandanna rather than a crown.

"*Perdón*," Javier interrupted the quiet conversation. The central tramp, with the bearing of freight-yard aristocracy, raised his eyebrows to consider the two brothers, then nodded his head. Recognized, Javier continued, "Piedras Negras. How do we find the train that goes there?"

"Piedras Negras," the tramp repeated, giving the problem his consideration. "On the border with Texas?"

"That's right."

"There is no train to Piedras Negras." He returned his cigarette, a long filter-tip, to his mouth.

"No trains?"

"Go to Paredón. There you can catch a train for Piedras Negras."

"And how do we get to Paredón?"

"See the third train over?" The tramp pointed. "I think it will go there." He glanced at his companions for confirmation. "Look on the side of the boxcars. There's a white cardboard tag that says where the car is going. Look at that. Then you know."

"And when does it leave?" Javier asked.

"Who knows?" The man flicked the cigarette. "Ask someone who works for the railroad."

"They will say?"

"Why not? What do they care?"

Javier and Juan crawled back over two trains to check the third. To the east the sky was growing light, but still they struck matches to read "Paredón" scrawled on the cardboard sticker. A man with a large oilcan going from car to car told them the train wouldn't leave till about ten in the morning, so they started toward the tramps. As they climbed from the last train, they saw the symmetrical three strolling away on the tracks. Javier and Juan walked to the edge of the freight yard where they sat down at the end of a line of immobilized boxcars that had been cut with windows and doors to make living quarters. Below the yard, they could see into a small tract of shoebox-shaped cement houses with chain-link fences, and an adjoining concrete-slab playground. Lights were coming on in the houses. Women came out to feed animals, to throw a dishpan of water into the yard, to walk to the corner *colmado* to buy breakfast; men left for work; children in uniforms left for school. On the far side of the freight yard, the sheer jut of the Sierra Madres came out gray against the pale blue sky.

"*¡Mira!*" Juan said looking back toward the trains. "A woman."

Javier turned and saw a couple walking across the tracks. The man was carrying a can of beer and wore a dirty T-shirt that sagged with the weight of his stomach. The woman carried a can of pineapple juice and had black hair that fell in waves to the shoulders of her magenta pantsuit. They both drank from the cans as though they were walking through a garden party rather than a freight yard. After watching for a moment, Javier decided: "It's a boy with long hair. A woman wouldn't come here."

"*No, hombre,*" Juan protested. "Look at her body, her clothes, the way she walks. I know a woman."

"*Maricón,*" Javier suggested.

"No," Juan shook his head. "No queer can fool me."

"Perhaps not," Javier said, watching them disappear behind a train. "I wonder where they're going."

A locomotive backed down the tracks before them, connected with a string of cars, and trudged back. "*A Tampico*," a brakeman shouted the train's destination to them as it passed.

"*A Paredón*," Javier shouted as he and Juan waved to the man.

At nine-thirty, they climbed down the embankment to the playground and drank from a water fountain before going to find a place on the train. Avoiding boxcars, they walked along the tracks till they came to an open wagon. They climbed the ladder and jumped in at the feet of the couple still sipping beer and pineapple juice while reclining on the side of a pile of coal. "*¡Ay, señor, mira!*" the woman exclaimed coquettishly to Juan as he took in her low-cut flowered blouse, chain necklace, and long fingernails that directed his attention to the fresh pile of human excrement on the floor at the end of the car. Shocked, Juan looked at her again and noticed the stubble above her upper lip. "I didn't want you to step in it," she smirked.

The two brothers scrambled over the coal to the far end of the wagon, where they sat on the metal siding. In the string of wagons behind theirs, other riders waited to leave for Paredón. A locomotive backed past, then returned pulling a long line of petroleum tankers like giant silver capsules on wheels. "*A Paredón*," a man on the train announced to the waiting riders as it rolled by. "*A Paredón*." Seeing the others abandon the train, Javier and Juan climbed down from the wagon, walked along beside a moving tank car, and pulled up on the ladder that curved over the metal bulge to the small platform surrounding the tank valve. Sulfurous-smelling crude oil splattered on the hot metal stuck to their hands and between their fingers as they climbed to the platform ringed by a metal barricade. Leaning against the railing, they stood on the platform and watched the stationary trains, which appeared to be rolling past, then the density of trash and shacks thin along the tracks as they moved out of the yards and into the desert.

The train gained velocity as it headed west. Fresh desert air blew away the smell of oil; a man on horseback briefly chased along the tracks. Jagged peaks of rock rose up out of the desert to the south like icebergs out of the ocean. Above, flat puzzle pieces of cloud pushed their gray shadows across the white, equally flat desert floor. Javier smiled broadly at Juan and pulled his ball cap snug. *"Tengo hambre,"* he shouted with the wind. I'm hungry.

Juan answered the smile. "Me too," he called, shaking his hair back in the wind.

"¡Mira!" Javier called and pointed with his chin. Juan turned, and on the tank car behind theirs, saw the couple standing together, leaning against the rail. The young man looked ecstatic holding up his can of juice as if to drink, his long black hair blowing out behind. His companion holding the beer can looked merely content.

"How long do you think those cans have been empty?" Juan called.

Javier smiled, shaking his head. *"La pareja dispareja."* The unmatched pair.

The train stuck to the floor beneath the sheer northern face of the Sierra Madres. Toward midday, the desert phased into a zone of dissolution where deep and rounded pits had fed an alluvial flow of frozen salt. The train followed the crystalline stream until it terminated in a salt flat trisected by branches of railroad. Among the branches were scattered the bare necessities of Paredón.

As soon as the train stopped, Javier and Juan got down from the tank car and crossed to an adobe wall of houses indented by pastel doors shut against the heat. Except for an occasional inorganic clank from the railroad, the town was silent. They drank at a water spigot beneath a cedar, then rinsed their shirts in the water and cupped it onto their dry, salty skin.

"*Los novios*," Javier wondered, looking out at the tank cars. "Where did they go?"

"The other way."

Nothing moved in Paredón except the heat waves. They waited for a clue of departure, then braced themselves to cross to the small railroad station on the far side of the tracks. Quiet clicking came from the telegraph as they climbed the ramp to the covered loading dock. The man inside said the train would come soon—in an hour, more or less. They sat down to wait in the shade at the end of the dock. A dry breeze blew from the desert; the cement was cool. Slipping, they fell into cool, twitching dreams of escape.

When the train came, they pushed aside the webby sleep and climbed into an open car filled with reddish clay pellets. Two riders, heads tucked away from the sun beneath their arms, lay sprawled on their stomachs in the car behind. The train broke the silence of Paredón, and, once again, Juan and Javier watched as the desert ticked past.

"What would this be?" Javier mused, turning over a compressed globe of the baked clay.

"Who knows?" Juan picked up a piece and looked at it. "But I wish we could eat it." He tossed the lump at a passing telegraph pole and yawned. Javier watched the clay sail wide of the pole, then picked up a piece and threw. Both unsuccessful, they took turns throwing until the line of poles peeled off from the tracks, out of range.

Javier tried to sleep by pressing himself against the clay but could never quite lose the intensity of the sun on his back to the lulling sound and motion of the train. He listened to Juan's quavering, daydreaming voice making up and fitting together a song about a young man from Jalisco, *macho* and brave, who left home for *el norte*. Crouched over on his haunches, idly handling the lumps of clay, Juan sang tunelessly to himself of all the broken hearts he left behind, the sadness, the hard journey to San Antonio, and of the *señoritas* he would find and the car he would have.

Annoyed by the droning song and Juan's daydream, Javier raised his head. "Better sing about work in San Antonio," he said. "That's what you're going for." Juan scowled at him, resentful that his daydream was disturbed, then lay down to try to sleep.

They watched the sun's descent, impatient for any sign that time was passing, that they might be nearing their destination. In the car behind, one of the young men had moved to the front, and, paying no attention to Juan and Javier, looked out at the desert. After a while, Javier walked back across the clay pellets and sat down on the opposite side of the coupling. They nodded, and Javier, noticing the other man sleeping and a plastic net shopping bag, shouted, "Where are you going?"

"San Antonio," he shouted. Small, thin, he was about twenty years old. His eyes were set too wide in his face and gave him a startled look. His mouth had a tense set.

"Me too," Javier answered.

"First time?"

Javier shook his head. "And you?"

"First time this way," the young man answered. "Before I had papers and went with friends in a car."

"Papers?"

"Forged." He grimaced, remembering. "Two nights ago in San Antonio I went out to the bars and left my papers at home. I stayed too late, till the bars closed, and walking home, the cops stopped me. No papers, so they kick me across the border. Here I am with nothing and have to walk."

"That's bad luck," Javier offered.

"It's what I get for drinking. But after work, I get sad at night. What else is there?"

"How long were you there?" Javier asked.

"Six months, this second time. I wanted to stay longer and save money to bring back. Work there, live in Mexico. If you don't save something, you're just as poor as if you never went."

"What kind of work?"

"Welding. I can get work whenever I want. That's what the boss says."

"That's good."

"But listen," he shouted to Javier. "Have you come this way before? Is it very hard?"

"It isn't easy. If it's very hard depends on the luck." Tired of shouting, Javier pointed at his throat, frowned, and shouted, "When the train stops, we can talk." He smiled, got up, and walked back to Juan.

The pallid moon rose to the east. The sun sank in the west. As Javier and Juan watched the tilt of celestial mechanics, the sun swelled to an enormous round orange, and then, its lower rim slipping behind a skim of clouds, became a flat disk dropping into a slot.

At ten o'clock the train stopped in Ciudad Frontera. Carnival lights of an oil refinery shone in the distance; nearby, dimly lit adobe huts lined an unpaved street. Seeing the two other riders going toward the corner store, Javier and Juan climbed down and walked up the rutted street until they found the communal water spigot. Thirst quenched, empty stomachs slightly bloated by the water, they walked back past the store where the other two stood drinking sodas in the doorway. "*¿Qué tal?*" the one in the white T-shirt greeted. His companion a man in his early thirties with gray hair, a slight paunch, and an untroubled face—nodded cordially. He would have looked upper class had the whites of his eyes not had a liverish cast.

"So-so," Javier said as he noticed they carried the net plastic bag.

"Do you mind if we ride with you?" the younger one asked. Javier said it would be fine.

Walking back to the train, Armando introduced himself and said his older friend was Toño. They had met on the train before Paredón; it was chance they were traveling together. After they had climbed into the car and settled down on the clay pellets, Toño began taking food out of the bag. "Might as well eat while we wait," he said.

Javier and Juan froze in the dark.

"There's plenty for everyone," Toño said, sensing their discomfort, and, without waiting for a response, passed around a small stack of tortillas, a lump of dry white cheese, and a bottle of hot sauce. While they ate, Toño said it was his first trip to Texas. He had not only a wife and two children to support, but younger brothers and sisters to educate. His parents had squandered their money to send him to seminary to become a priest, and now he felt some obligation to the others. Not having a trade, Texas seemed the only way.

"You were going to be a priest?" Javier asked.

"I was very young," Toño said mildly.

"Identification," Armando was telling Juan. "As soon as you get to San Antonio, that's what you need. Identification and the Social Security number. Find a Chicano who isn't working and you can use his number. Then go to the Alamo. Across the street, there's an office with a big sign that says 'ID.' There they'll make the card for you."

Javier listened to Armando with some amusement, knowing that Juan had no idea about Social Security nor what or where the Alamo was. But recognizing the tone of voice that needs to know and tell, he didn't interrupt.

The train lurched forward, and refinery lights fell behind. They passed slowly through the town and into the desert split by the forlorn airhorn. Wheels clicked faster at rail junctures. Gray pads of cactus, drab mesquite leaves, and steel rails glittered white and silver in the moonlight. The dry breeze turned cold as the train rolled north through the night.

Toward dawn, the lights of Piedras Negras came into view. Not caring what came next, only that they get off the train and out of the chill breeze, they sat and watched the shacks, and the parallel railroad tracks that led to the yard. As the sky turned gray, the train, without finale or climax, slowed to a silent halt on a freight-yard siding.

"We're here?" Toño asked with surprise.

"Piedras Negras," Javier said. They got down from the wagon and walked north through the edge of town toward the river. At the first street light, they saw that their faces and hands, like those of minstrels, were coated with the black exhaust from the locomotive, and their hair stood as stiff as steel wool.

Where the street came to a dead end, heaps of garbage cascaded down through the mesquite trees to the river. By first light, they could see across the brown water to a green and manicured golf course in Eagle Pass. Juan picked up a long stick and walked along the river, prodding the bottom.

"It's deep," Javier assured him, noticing that the water still lapped over the green grass on the riverbank.

"But it's calm," Armando interjected.

"There are currents you don't see," Javier replied.

They started through town to go the fifteen miles upriver to Jiménez, where Javier thought they might find either rapids to cross or someone who would help them. In a small village, the chances seemed better. By eight, they were out on the road west. The morning grew hot; their sweat ran black with diesel exhaust. At ten, a farmer stopped his pickup and let them climb in back. They rode to Jiménez, where they got down, walked through the patchwork of cultivated fields, into the wide flat river bottom shaded by stands of oak and pecan, and through the rustling green canebrake with its dry, snapping undergrowth. The cane parted, and they stood on the riverbank before an expanse of water.

"Too bad Moisés isn't with us," Toño sighed.

"Moisés?" Juan frowned at him. "Who is that?"

"Moisés," Toño repeated. "You didn't see *Los Diez Mandatos* with Charlton Heston?"

Juan shook his head. The others listened.

"Moisés was the one leading the little Israelitos out of Egypt. The Pharaoh, this big guy, and his army were chasing them, and when they got to the sea, Moisés made the water part. The Israelitos walked across on the dry bottom, but when the Pharaoh and his army followed, the sea closed and they all drowned."

Juan looked impressed but doubtful. "How did this Moisés make the sea open?"

"God helped him," Toño explained.

"God?"

"It's from the Bible," Javier said and started up the river.

Single file, they followed Javier along the riverbank till he came to a halt at a small, sandy shoal. He sat down, took off his boots, then stood and began to undress. Nude, he waded into the water, sat down, and turned to look at the three watching him. "Going to swim?" Armando asked.

"Bathe," Javier said. Seeing the point, the others took off their clothes and followed him into the water. Using sand, they scrubbed the greasy soot off their skin, washed their hair as best they could, and then got their clothes to rinse. When they had spread their clothing out on the grass and cane, they got back in the water to float.

"Couldn't we swim across?" Toño asked, looking at the far bank, its fringe of cane at the bottom of a dirt cliff.

"Not and keep our boots and the food dry," Javier said. "But somewhere the river spreads out into rapids where we can wade across. We have to wait till someone comes who can tell us where."

Part IV

DON CHITTIM SAW a flash of white in the cane. He trained his binoculars on the spot, focused the lenses to bring in a thin young Mexican in a white T-shirt. The white faded into the cane and in its place appeared another young Mexican in a pale blue shirt. "Get the shirts," Chittim said to Adams, who lay on the bank beside him scanning the far side of the river with his binoculars. "A blue and a white."

"Where you have 'em?" Adams asked, still staring through the glasses.

"Now I don't," Chittim said. "They're moving west on that little path along the bank. Look upriver from the big tree just before the island. You might get 'em in a gap in the cane."

Adams looked over his binoculars to spot the tree; then, walking on his elbows, he repositioned himself to train his binoculars on the path. The last light was fading fast, and, to the west, the sky was already pink where the sun had set. A pall of smoke hung low over the riverbank; downriver on the Mexican side, fires glowed red in the dry undergrowth of canebrake. "Do you think they're spottin' their group to cross?" Adams said beneath the binoculars.

"Could be. If they cross anywhere around here, they're comin' through the rapids."

"Just two of 'em, you say?"

"That's all I saw. But then it could have been just the last two walking in a line, or the others could be laid up somewhere waitin'." He squirted tobacco juice on the ground in front of him, then raised up on his hands and knees. "Think I'll just sneak down to the water in case they try and cross."

He took off his straw Stetson, stashed his binoculars in the hat, and crept as stealthily as his girth allowed down a large gully to the riverbank. The sound of rushing water became clear as he walked a trail into the canebrake that rimmed the bank. At the main path up from the river, he sat down to wait. The river whispered, blooped, and gurgled over the stony bottom. Frogs croaked, crickets chirped, there was the recurring sound of water dripping. Chittim leaned back on his elbows to see the first stars shine like diamonds through the leafy fringe of cane; then, sure he could hear anyone climbing out of the river, he lay flat on his back, hands cupped behind his head to watch the sky turn pale with moonlight. "Hope they don't stampede me," he said quietly to himself, then unsnapped his holster and adjusted the walkie-talkie attached to his belt. He had considered the service revolver excess baggage until the year before, when a Mexican boatman had started shooting at him with a rifle. That had changed his attitude.

Javier stood with his legs spread wide to brace himself against the rushing water. The current felt strong enough to wash him downstream if he raised either foot from the rough, rocky bottom. Behind him on the bank, the others stood next to a man carrying a rifle and two little boys trailing along. Before Javier, a path of moonlight led across the rapids to a small island midway in the stream. He leaned against the current, raised his right foot, and slid it to a higher foothold in the sharp stones. Slowly, crablike, he edged his way up to shallow water. *"No se puede,"* he hissed to the man. It can't be done.

"Sí, se puede," the man objected. Stocky, barefoot like the two little boys, he looked impatient. One of the boys had started to cling to his leg and complain about being hungry. "Two crossed here this afternoon," the man insisted.

"But not in the dark," Javier said, taking his pants from Juan as he climbed up on the bank. Javier stepped into the pants, then sat down to pull on his boots.

They had come across the man with the rifle and his two little boys earlier in the afternoon. The man had said there had been no rain, but as usual, the gringos had let water out of the dam upriver. When Javier asked about a place to cross, the man offered to show the way. Implicit was a fee.

Javier didn't know how much Toño and Armando had, but reasoned that as the man was armed, he would get what he could. Having nothing, Javier and Juan had nothing to lose.

"I could take you now," the man said, "but these boys are hungry. Tonight I'll show you a place to sleep, and tomorrow I take you across myself." Without waiting for an answer, he turned and started away from the river. At a small dirt road that led out of the smoke-filled canebrake, he stopped, waved them ahead, and walked behind with the rifle. They followed the road through the river bottom, past two fields of moonlight, and into a grove of scrub oak. "Here, you can sleep," he indicated a cleared path with the barrel of the rifle. "No one will bother you till I come back tomorrow."

"When will you come?" Javier asked.

"The first thing in the morning, we'll cross." He turned and padded out of the grove and across a moonlit field, the two little boys in tow.

Left alone, they cleared the ground with their boots and lay down to rest. Above, the moon was circled by three rings of haze.

"Chittim, you go off to sleep down there?" Adams' voice crackled in the canebrake. Chittim sat up, detached the walkie-talkie from his belt, and pulled the antenna. "Just about," he answered. "You think those ol' boys chickened out?"

"Looks like it," Adams said. "River's runnin' pretty fast to cross in the dark." Pause. "Why don't we try somewhere else? I think the ticks are startin' to get after me up here."

"Whatever you say," Chittim agreed.

Javier woke at sunrise. The others got up, and Toño distributed tortillas and cheese while they waited for the man with the rifle. When he didn't come, they lay back down to wait and fell soundly asleep. They slept till midmorning, when the growing heat and the flies and gnats that crawled across their faces investigating lips, nostrils, and tear ducts woke them. Groggy from the hot sleep, they waited till midday before giving up on the man and starting for the river.

By daylight, the river crossing looked more plausible. A narrow channel separated them from the gravel island. The water ran deep and swift for a width of four or five feet, but beyond the island, the rapids looked uniformly flat and shallow.

Javier stripped off his clothes and started in at the narrowest part of the channel to test the water. Directly across from the island, he waded in up to his waist, took another step, lost his footing, and was swept floundering and splashing downstream until he was able to grab hold of the weedy bank at the end of the island. "You made it," Toño called when Javier had hobbled back up the island.

"Barely," Javier replied. "And I never would have carrying my boots and clothes."

"I'm going to try," Armando called to Javier, then sat down to take off his shoes. He stripped off his clothes and walked upstream on the riverbank, gingerly picking his way through the weeds until he was above the island. At a small clump of willow, he held onto a limb, lowered himself into the water, and, feet spread wide, edged out till the water was rushing about his waist, then above his stomach. Suddenly, his hands held above the water, he went scooting across the channel at an angle, coming to rest on the bank directly in front of Juan and Toño.

Javier smiled and looked impressed standing on the island above Armando. "How did you do that?" he asked.

"Let the water take you," Armando instructed. "Get an angle on the current and keep your feet flat on the bottom. The rocks hurt, but you don't lose your balance." Armando climbed out, and they both went to the head of the island to recross the channel.

Reluctantly, Juan and Toño received instructions. All of them wrapped their clothes in a tight ball to carry in one hand, leaving the other hand free for boots or shoes. Armando, more confident than the rest, had volunteered to carry the plastic net bag as well, and was just leading the way into the water when they heard the drone of an airplane. *"La migra,"* Javier said. Naked, they rushed away from the river and into the cane, where they squatted down to wait. The drone grew louder till downriver a plane came into view above the riverbanks. "Get low," Javier called. The plane seemed to hum slowly along till it got close, then roared overhead.

"Did it see?" Armando asked.

"If it circles, yes," Javier answered. "If it doesn't, perhaps." The roar was quickly fading to a drone. Javier cautiously stood to watch the disappearing tail.

"It's not coming back," Armando said with relief. "It didn't see us."

"Or it just didn't need a second look."

"What difference does it make," Toño asked, "till we're on the other side?"

"If they saw us," Javier answered, "someone will be there to meet us." Still furtive, he picked up his boots and clothing and stepped out of the cane.

They walked back to the river, and Armando started across. When he had made it safely to the island, Javier began. Each went in turn until they had crossed the narrow channel without mishap. They hobbled over the rocky island to the wide stretch of rapids. "Easy," Armando declared the crossing. The first thirty feet of water was no more than five or six inches deep, and they started across together. Looking down the line at all of them naked, limping pathetically across the rocks, Toño cracked, "the invaders," then slipped and landed on his seat, still holding boots and clothes above his head. Everyone laughed while Javier and Juan helped him up.

As the water ran deeper, each step became a tense negotiation against the swift current. A misstep or a moment's too-long hesitation was enough to be knocked over. Armando went ahead. He reached the bank, and the others followed until only Juan was left in the water. He stood frowning at the swirl and appeared to be stuck.

"Keep moving," Armando encouraged.

"I can't," he answered with obvious annoyance.

The three stood watching until Javier called, "If you fall

in and get wet, it's okay. But come on before we get caught."

Realizing that he wasn't on the brink of disaster, Juan regained his nerve and proceeded across the river.

They dressed quickly. Toño filled the milk container he had brought in his bag, and they climbed up the dirt bank into a canebrake. The first small clearing they came to, Javier vetoed and pushed on till the cane was solid. "Hide yourselves," he advised.

"How long will we be here?" Armando asked.

"One or two in the morning. When there's less chance of being seen." Javier got down on hands and knees to crawl through the cane, weaving snakelike till he was out of view.

It was quiet for a while in the cane, then there was more rustling and crackling. Juan's voice floated through, rose and fell, suppressed a giggle. He was talking to Armando and Toño about *las rukas*—chicks—and trying to make them laugh. Javier listened to the lazy, aimless voice till it barked with an uncontrolled laugh. "Juan!" Javier hissed. "This isn't a game."

The talk paused, then continued in a slow murmur.

They dozed. The afternoon passed. When Javier woke, he realized that the other three had moved into the clearing. As they hadn't been caught and he himself was uncomfortable, he decided to join them. As soon as he moved, the sound of voices died away. The lull lasted as he crawled out, and the conversation didn't resume once he sat down. Shadows from the cane fell across the open ground, and a breeze blew from the river. Finally, Armando began. "We've been talking."

"And?"

"We want to go when the sun sets. It's darkest then before the moon is high."

Javier looked at Toño for confirmation and then at Juan. "Fine. As soon as the sun sets."

They ate, then waited. The sky went through its blue declension to a final shade of green; the moon, orange like a Gulf sign, appeared above the cane.

"Two things," Javier said in a hushed voice. "Don't make any noise, and try not to leave tracks. The river runs north-south here so we will have to head eastward before cutting to the north. For the first six or seven miles there are little farms and houses. Here we have to be very careful."

They turned their backs on the river and started walking quietly in the shadow of cane. The brake filled a large ravine that led them, within cover, to a barbed-wire fence and an open field. Beyond the field they saw headlights moving from east to west on a highway. "This way," Javier said and turned into the cane, automatically avoiding the field. The cane thickened, its dry undergrowth crashed and snapped, and, as they pushed forward, the ground dropped from beneath them, so that they were left hanging on the side of the ravine. "Wait!" Javier finally called above the loud thrashing that filled the ravine. Suspended, they waited. "It's too thick," he declared and started pulling himself out.

From the fence, they considered the freshly plowed field. Low, it was still untouched by the moonlight; its darkness had the quality of shadow and the depth of contrast. "When we cross," Javier whispered, "try to step in the tracks before you. If it looks like one person crossed, maybe they won't bother to chase us."

He stepped on a wire attached at the post and jumped over. A cloud of powder puffed up as he landed and sank slowly to his shins. "*¡Por Dios!*" he staggered to maintain balance. The field was not only freshly plowed, but also newly cleared. Root plows had turned over a foot of fine river silt, creating a dry mire until the first planting.

A cloud of dust followed them as they hurried across the field, leaving not so much a track as a ditch in their path. Halfway, they came to an irrigation canal of water that forced them to turn to the west. Anticipating a way to cross, they followed the canal to a long rise that separated the field from the highway. The canal ran parallel to the rise and the highway, and each step they took, took them farther out of the way. Frustrated, they kept walking until they saw the lights of a small house on the opposite side of the canal. Abruptly, Javier came to a halt and turned to the others. "We're in a trap," he said. "We have to wade the canal."

Armando, Juan, and Toño looked down at the muddy canal and the steep, weedy bank on the opposite side. "There has to be a bridge farther up," Juan objected. "They have to bring tractors in."

"Dogs at the house will bark."

"We can circle out into the field away from the house," Juan persisted.

"No," Javier said, a note of panic rising in his voice. "If there's a bridge, *inmigración* will be there waiting for us. We're in a trap. I know it."

"It's not deep," Toño said mildly from the bank, which he

had gone down to investigate. "But it's going to be like quicksand."

Javier didn't bother to reply, but sat down to take off his boots. He stuffed socks in boots, took off his pants, and started for the canal. Armando and Toño looked at each other, then did the same. The three had started into the canal, their feet and legs making loud suction noises in the slick mud, before Juan acquiesced and started to take off his boots. By the time they had reached the far side, they had sunk to above their knees and had to pull themselves out by grabbing the weeds and grass on the bank. Crossing last, Juan found the bottom sinking even faster beneath his feet. He strained and splashed harder; the mud sucked louder. "Hey," he hissed, just out of reach of the bank. "I'm stuck."

"Be still," Javier hissed back and started down the bank. He reached out, took Juan's hand, and with one long, sucking noise, pulled him out. Through deep weeds, they scrambled up the rise into the moonlight. Their underwear glowed white; the mud on their legs shone like black stockings.

"How do we get dressed?" Toño said, looking down at his black legs and feet.

"Just get it off your feet," Javier said, ripping up and knotting handfuls of grass. "The rest you can wash off later." Tension was making his voice jerky. They were sitting within view of the highway, and though the headlights didn't hit them, Javier knew it was possible for a Border Patrol car to pass and beam the roadside with a spotlight. He ground dry dirt into the mud on his feet and buffed them until they began to feel fairly clean. By the time Juan got to the top of the rise, Javier had slid his pants on over his wet, muddy legs and was putting on his boots. "Hurry up," he snapped at Juan. "Hurry up," he kept saying.

Crouching low, the four approached the highway. At the fence, they lay in the dark waiting for a break in the traffic. A diesel truck passed, its lights sweeping away the dark, its drone winding out to leave the road in silence. "Now," Javier called. Each climbed a post in the fence, ran up the embankment, crossed the pavement, and dropped into the far ditch just as car lights appeared on the horizon.

Across the fence in front of them lay a low, scooped-out pasture bisected by a shallow gully and an eight-foot cyclone fence. The fence and gully terminated at a drainage tube beneath the highway. Beyond the gully and the far half of the pasture, a house sat next to the highway within the glow of a large security light. Avoiding the exposure of the house and the necessity of climbing up to the highway to get past the drainage tube, Javier started over the fence and up the pasture, staying on the western side of the gully.

The gully led abruptly to another embankment. At the top, they confronted a canal running west which, as far as they could see, blocked their northern advance. "No," Juan said, seeing Javier weigh the alternatives of crossing the canal or going back to the house with its security light. "I'm not going through more water."

"We're rats in a trap," Javier remarked and started back toward the highway.

Midway in the pasture, its cover of shadow shrinking beneath the moon like fog beneath the sun, Javier barked "Down!" and they all fell to the ground. A pale-green-and-white sedan cruising along the highway slowed, then pulled to a stop above the drainage tube. They could hear a car door open and close, and, peeping over their forearms, could see a man with a flashlight climb down the bank to the drainage tube. He poked the beam of light into the dark pipe and then played it out through the dry gully, forcing them to flatten themselves closer to the ground, squeeze their eyes shut, and look away. Afraid to look, they lay frozen till the car door opened and slammed shut again.

"*La migra*," Javier said as the car drove slowly away. "They've seen our track from the river and are looking for us."

"What can we do?" Toño asked.

"Nothing." Javier stood and headed for the highway.

They grouped at the bottom of the embankment; then Javier climbed up to the roadbed above the drainage pipe to drop down on the far side of the gully and the cyclone fence. A car passed, then a truck. Juan climbed up and dropped down to join Javier. Then Armando and finally Toño. Together, the four walked quickly toward the house. No lights showed in the windows, but as they approached they could hear a dog begin to bark. They hesitated a moment at the edge of the bright pool of light, then ran heavily in their boots past the front of the house to cut north into the fields beyond.

The dog's bark followed them into the dark and across the field. Slowing to a hard, fast walk, they crossed another field and came to a raised road of white caliche. In the moonlight, the road shone like ribbon running across the dark fields. Javier hesitated, then stepped up on the road. "What about tracks?" Armando asked as he and the others followed.

"There's no way to cross through here without leaving tracks," Javier answered. "It doesn't make that much difference if footprints are on the road or in a field." And so they followed the road. The dry mud on their legs began to crack and itch, pulling at the hair. To the southeast, the lights of Piedras Negras and Eagle Pass glowed; the sounds of the highway fell behind. They walked hard until they came to another irrigation canal, where the road turned west. Frustrated, yet committed to the road, they followed until they saw a small bridge that crossed the canal. The bridge, however, was guarded by a lighted shack and a street lamp at the intersection of two caliche roads. Javier slowed the pace and they approached with caution. At regular intervals, the dead roar of canned laughter poured out of the house.

"What now?" Armando whispered.

Javier considered the drainage canal that ran along the road and saw that they would not only have to cross it to get into the field, but also to get out. "Take a chance," he said.

Slowly, they walked toward the bridge and into the street light. Above the house and the sound of television, they could hear a cottonwood rustle mysteriously, then a small dog began to yap with hysteria. Barking, it rushed out to meet them as they turned across the bridge. Toño leaned down as if to pick up a stone and brought the mongrel to a dancing, barking halt at the edge of the road. A man inside the house shouted at the dog but failed to come to the door. The four walked quickly past the house and the old Ford parked in front and were out of the light of the street lamp walking east into the white moonlight when the tempo of the television's roar signaled a commercial and the man came out on the porch. He shouted at the dog again, then walked out to the road. "Hello," he called at their receding backs, then leaned down into the car to switch on the headlights.

"Good-bye," Javier called back in his best English, not stopping in the beam of light. The man watched them a moment, then switched off the lights and walked back into the house.

They ran east on the white road until they came to a road that led north. In the distance, they could see the dark silhouette of a brushy-looking ridge that promised an end to the open exposure of the fields. They trotted on till the road brought them to a mesquite-filled pasture and an old wooden gate. Without hesitation, they climbed the gate and, somewhat relieved by the shadows of the mesquite trees, walked at a fast pace up the sandy lane. The sight of a barn slowed them, but, as there were no lights or a house, they proceeded through the barnyard, into the brush, and on toward the ridge. The ground made a sharp dip beneath the ridge, and the density and depth of brush, weeds, and cactus made a quantum leap. Sweating from the run and the sudden closeness but propelled by the prospect of cover, they staggered into the brush, then started up the ridge. The ridge was steep like a wall. The brush clawed back as they clawed their way to the top. Hand over hand they went until Javier felt a flat, cleared space and pulled himself up. As he stood, he made the disconcerting discovery that he was again on a road, which ran along the top of the ridge for what appeared to be miles in either direction. Across the road, a fifteen-foot-wide canal separated them from the brush country to the north. They had climbed the embankment to the main canal from the river.

"This is why they haven't chased us," Javier said as the others climbed up on the road. "We're in another trap. All they have to do is wait for us at either end."

"Isn't there a bridge?" Armando asked.

"That's where they'll wait."

They stared hopelessly across the canal at the brush. "Couldn't we swim?" Toño asked, looking down at the reflected moonlight in the swiftly moving water.

"One of us would drown." Javier sighed heavily and asked Toño for the water bottle in his plastic bag. They each drank, Toño refilled the bottle from the canal, and they started west away from the glow of Piedras Negras and Eagle Pass. Below them, as they went, they could see the man-made regularity of the embankment and the checkerboard of irrigated fields stretching away toward the Rio Grande. They walked on until they saw a distant flash of white lights followed immediately by a flash of red. "That's it," Javier declared. "That's the bridge."

As they drew closer, they could hear the spin of pickup tires on pavement, then saw the white-and-red flash of light going in the opposite direction.

"The canal goes under the road," Armando surmised.

"That's where they're waiting," Javier said and came to a halt.

"Should we go back?" Toño asked.

"It will be the same at the other end." Javier moved over to the edge of the embankment and squatted down next to the border of weeds. The others followed and they sat watching for another flash of light. "If we could see them first, we might have a chance. We could wait till the shift changed."

"Or maybe they go to sleep," Juan suggested.

"Follow me and we'll see," Javier said. "But don't make any noise and hide yourself against these weeds."

Bent over, single file they crept thirty feet up the road, then squatted by the weeds again to see if they had been spotted. When a flashlight didn't reveal them, they made another advance and again waited to be caught. They moved toward the bridge in a series of diminishing progressions, waiting, listening. A car occasionally crossed the bridge; they could hear the water running smoothly in the canal. At twenty feet, they could see both sides of the bridge. A last advance and they were at the edge of the road. They waited patiently, listening for a cough, voices, some indication of the Border Patrol. The minutes passed slowly until Javier turned to the others, shrugged his shoulders, and stood up. They crossed the bridge, trotted down into the ditch to the fence, and climbed a wooden stile to jump into brush country.

At the Border Patrol station in Eagle Pass, the computer console clacked out four hits on the seismic sensor buried beneath the left leg of the stile. Garza, the PI monitoring the console, tore off the paper tape and walked over to a series of maps displayed beneath glass. Each map depicted a small area where a network of sensors had been planted. Estimated times required for a man to walk from one sensor to the next were printed on the maps next to slots where the actual times of sensor readings were temporarily marked on the glass with a wax pen. By comparing the actual and the estimated times it was possible to distinguish between wandering livestock and the direct and steady pace of a man. Garza marked the four hits next to the stile and noticed that four had registered earlier in the network on the canal road and next to the bridge. The elapsed times between the different sensors were erratic, but the fact that there were four made it fairly certain that they were illegal aliens, the other options being cows, coyotes, and rattlesnakes—none of which traveled in groups of four. Garza was checking the network due south where earlier in the evening he had had what appeared to be a group of four when he saw Chittim pass the doorway. "Chittim," he called.

"Yeah?" he stuck his head in the doorway.

"Didn't you and Adams have the river watch at the rapids between Quemado and Normandy this week?"

"That's right," Chittim stepped into the room.

"How was it tonight?"

"No luck at the rapids but got four trying to cross the highway. Then we had to mess with some wets that Customs picked up. They've got the worst damn paperwork."

"Looks like four got past you somehow. I got four squawks on the highway sensors above the rapids and just had readings from what must be the same ones at the canal and the ranch road to Spofford."

"Oh yeah?" Chittim said, interested.

"Four here," Garza ticked the end of the wax pen on the large area map, "and four here." He tapped the conjunction of the canal and the ranch road.

"Well, can't get 'em all."

"You think I ought to radio the boys out in that area?"

Chittim studied the map a moment. The second set of readings placed the Mexicans between the ranch road and the state highway that ran parallel about five miles apart up from the river highway to Spofford, fifteen miles away. "I wouldn't bother," Chittim said. "These wets'll get lined out on the road or on the lights to the radio antennae at Spofford. Either way, the boys on morning shift out there can pick 'em up. Just make sure they know."

For the first time since they crossed the river, Javier began to feel hopeful, yet he pushed them hard to get away from the highway, up a brush-covered rocky ridge, and east toward the full moon. After the open fields and the canals, the scratch and the pull of thorns were reassurance. They pushed on to the top of the ridge where they could see a set of red taillights mapping out the ranch road north, then continued east on the flat, scrubby ridge until the road was out of sight and the lights of Eagle Pass and Piedras Negras had come into view before turning north toward Spofford.

Each step was a release of tension; their pace increased and assumed the emotion of flight. The moon lit a cow path through the brush that traversed a series of ravines fluting the edge of the main ridge. Up the side of each ravine,

Javier marched briskly. Down, he ran with the pull of gravity. He didn't look back or stop until he heard Juan stumble on rocks behind him. "Break an ankle," he warned as Juan pulled himself up, "and we're finished."

A last ascent through a ravine took them up to the mesa top spread flat beneath the moon. Low, tight brush and cactus fell away to sparsely placed mesquite. Javier held the pace; the others gradually strung out behind until each walked alone. As the last of their tension ebbed, the walking became mechanical. Armando caught up with Juan and passed him. Then Toño. At a fence, they waited for Juan, but, before he could climb over, Javier had taken off.

Falling had knocked the last of the energy out of Juan. Moreover, it made him worry that he would fall again and be left; then he worried that he simply couldn't keep up. He could see Toño ahead of him in the brush, but no matter how hard he tried, he couldn't go any faster. He concentrated on each footstep to move his legs faster, but the effect was hypnotic. An acute lethargy overcame him that made holding eyelids up, much less moving legs, an act of concentration. Twice he stumbled as if he were falling asleep on his feet. His eyes began to itch with the hard moonlight.

If only Javier would stop, Juan thought, so that they could sleep. He didn't see why they had to keep rushing, and he began to resent the rapid pace. "*Jamás, jamás,*" he said to himself and swore that he would never again come to Texas. He thought of Javier somewhere in front and began to gather the wrongs, slights, insults that Javier had done him. Why, he wondered, had he let Javier bring him?

"Pssss!" he finally hissed at the others. Toño stopped, signaled Armando and Javier, and the three walked back for him.

"We'll rest," Javier anticipated Juan, "when the moon is straight up. Another hour." He took the water bottle from Toño, opened it, and gave it to Juan. "This is good walking at night but impossible for day. Here, they could see us for miles." Javier drank last, capped the bottle, and started north.

Juan measured the moon's ascent in footsteps. "Never again," he snarled at Javier when they finally came to a halt. "This is the last time." He lay down on the ground and slept immediately.

Javier, Toño, and Armando sat on the ground and drank from the water bottle. To the south, they could hear the nervous complaint of coyotes.

"Should we eat?" Toño offered.

"Later," Javier said. "We'll take a longer break." Feeling the muscles in his legs tighten, he got up and walked in a large, slow circle, then came back and nudged Juan with his boot. Juan jerked awake.

"You've slept. Let's go." Javier stood above Juan to see that he got up.

At the top of a long, gentle rise, Javier saw two vague red lights on the horizon. He watched to make sure the lights didn't move and waited for the others to catch up. "*Las antenas de Espoford*," he announced and pointed to the lights. "If we get to the other side by dawn, then we'll be safe."

They tracked on the red lights to the north, the glow of Eagle Pass and Piedras Negras to the southeast, and the moon above. To the west, an oil rig lighted green and white like a rocket ride at the carnival came into view. As they walked, they gradually came even with the rig, passed it, and left it behind, only to have it pop up again before them. The green-and-white lights seemed to precede or follow according to the compass direction they walked. If they angled to the east it was before them. If they faced to the west, it was behind. The red lights appeared and disappeared depending on slight variations in the landscape. Their emotions rose and fell with the lights.

The burden of lethargy that Juan carried spread to Toño. Toño slowed and fell into last place, stretching the line out. In front, Javier was aware of the drag of exhaustion but kept going. By sheer willpower, he was determined to pull the others along.

At a slight descent, the red lights disappeared. Before them, like a mirage, a two-story Victorian ranch house loomed on an exposure of limestone bedrock. Cattle troughs surrounded the house, and from a distance, the white ground appeared fly-specked. At a concrete trough, they drank and sat down to rest against its side. Toño got out food, they ate, and all went to sleep except Javier. To stay awake, he sat pulling the wads of dried mud from the hair on his legs and listened to their breathing. After ten minutes, he woke them. "¡Vámonos!" he said, getting to his feet. "We slept more than an hour." They looked at him groggily, then started to get up.

"It seemed like minutes," Armando sighed.

The red lights reappeared on the horizon and stayed there. As long as they could see the lights, they trudged forward. The moon slid in its western descent; their perception of time, like that of space, fluctuated as they walked. At times it seemed they had walked forever; at times it seemed like minutes.

The red lights disappeared again, and Juan threw himself to the ground. "*Ya no,*" he said. "Leave me here." Javier, Toño, and Armando said nothing and lay down on the ground. When Javier caught himself falling asleep, he jerked to, slept again, and then got up. Behind them, he could see the faint glow of Eagle Pass and Piedras Negras. When the others got up, Juan pointed at the southern lights. "Espoford," he said. "We're almost there."

"That's Piedras," Javier corrected him.

"You're confused," Juan said with certainty. "That's Espoford. We're too far away to see Piedras." Neither Toño nor Armando spoke, but Javier sensed that they agreed with Juan, that the glow of light was more convincing than his opinion. Incredulous, Javier looked at them, then wondered if he were somehow confused. The moon should be going down on his left, he reasoned. Facing the lights, it was to his right. "Espoford is that way," he pointed to the north. Without another word, he started walking. Behind him, he could hear them hesitate, then reluctantly follow. He didn't relax until the red lights came back into view.

The sleep helped and they walked hard. They crossed a fence—the first in hours—then came to a clearing and a smooth track next to another fence. They walked along the track until they realized that beyond lay a two-lane paved highway. They stood a moment at the fence to look at the asphalt, then started back through the clearing. Ahead, they could distinctly see the red antennae lights above the horizon.

Keeping the road in view, they moved through the thin cover of mesquite. The sky paled to the east; the moon hung low in the west. A breeze picked up and they heard a bird sing. From the south, the sound of a pickup rose in a precise arc, approached, and passed as they stood watching in the brush. The eastern sky turned bright blue, and, just as the red antennae lights came within reach, sunrise dimmed their promise.

Lee Feltner watched through the windshield as the sun turned the sky pink and blue. He held the steering wheel with his left hand, balanced a red plastic cup on the seat, and braced the plaid Thermos between his legs to twist the top off. "You sure you don't want some coffee, Jessie?"

Centeno said "No." Tall and lanky, he slouched against his door as if he wanted a pillow.

"Cookie?" Feltner suggested as he extricated one of the peanut-shaped peanut-butter cookies from the lunch his wife packed.

Centeno declined that also.

Feltner figured his wife would be peeved if she knew he started his lunch at sunrise, but he didn't see that it mattered. If it was a good day, he wouldn't have time to eat later. Neatly constructed, he sat perched behind the steering wheel eating cookies and drinking coffee. With his blond hair and blue eyes, he exuded an early-morning sense of well-being.

Dawn, according to Feltner, was about the best time of day, and he regretted having to share it with someone who would rather be at home in bed. He didn't mind training new PIs—that was part of his job—but it wasn't the same now that most of them were Mexicans from Houston or San Antonio. Or rather Chicanos, as he had learned to say. The race part didn't bother Feltner so much as the fact that so many came from the city. It just seemed backward to take a man who had never seen a windmill, didn't know what mesquite was, and couldn't get a gate open, and try to make a sign cutter out of him. Most of the older PIs, like Feltner, had grown up in small Texas towns and liked to hunt and fish. Not only did they take naturally to sign cutting, but they had plenty to say. If pressed hard enough, Feltner would admit that most of the new men caught on pretty well, but the Border Patrol wasn't the same. What with all the changes and Carter and Castillo causing a wetback stampede by talking about amnesty, Feltner had definitely started looking forward to mandatory retirement at fifty-five.

Feltner slowed the vehicle and turned east off the state highway onto a small sandy lane. "Got a road brushed out down here," he explained as he stopped the vehicle in front of the gate. "Might as well see what kind of sign we got."

Centeno opened the gate and they drove slowly down the lane, staring hard at the ground in the headlights. "Oh my," Feltner said and stepped on the brakes. "We got us a whole herd coming through here." He switched off the motor, and they got out to inspect the ground that in the headlights looked choppy with footprints. Hands on hips, Feltner approached the tracks. "Tennie runner," he said, and pointed out a clean tennis-shoe track with the toe of his right cowboy boot. "Got us a *guarache* worn tread," he indicated a foot-shaped tire imprint. "*Guarache* sidewall, a plain sole, another tennie runner, Guanajuato boot, ripple sole, *guarache*, Monterrey slipper." It began to sound like a strange incantation as he went slowly from footprint to footprint across the road to the fence.

"I guess these ol' boys are lined out along the highway by now," he said to Centeno. "If they knew what they was doin', they wouldn't travel in such a pack nor stay so close to the road. But then maybe this is their first time and they're scared."

"How old would you say these tracks are?" Centeno asked.

"Hard to say exactly," Feltner said as he took out a pad he carried in his shirt pocket and started making note of what he saw. "What sign looks like depends on the ground and the elements. Gives a lot of variables to calculate. Now these tracks have got age in them. You can tell that 'cause they're not real sharp." He stepped down on the sand, then stepped back to demonstrate. "See how sharp that looks. It almost shines at you. But these tracks—it's been a quiet night, no wind—I'd say they was put down early last night. And it could have been more than one group. Yes, sir, Jessie, it's hard to say exactly."

From the truck, Feltner radioed headquarters. After he had given their location and read the list of sign from the pad, he listened to the dispatcher. "That right? Well, goddog!" he said and listened again. "Okey-dokey. Ten-four."

"Caught a pack of seventeen north of here last night," he reported to Centeno. "Sounds like these ones were with 'em."

"Seventeen together," Centeno repeated.

"Sensors showed four more over at the ranch road and the canal." Feltner started the motor. "They're probably comin' our way."

They drove farther down the lane to turn around. Centeno got out, opened the tailgate, and pulled a large tractor tire attached to a chain out of the back. The tire fell flat on the road, Centeno got in, and they drove back up the road and out the gate, leaving a clean slate for the next PIs to check.

On the highway, they made good time till Feltner figured they were within four or five miles of Spofford. Slowing, he cut across the left-hand side of the road, and drove through the grassy ditch and onto a brushed-out strip next to the fence. Centeno got out to drop the tractor tire out the back again; Feltner switched on the spotlight just outside his window, focused it on a strip that had been cleared within the fence, and told Centeno to watch the strip in the headlights.

They drove slowly along the fence line, Feltner with his chin resting on his arm in the windowsill watching the ground inside the fence line, Centeno watching the ground ahead in the headlights. Stare as he might, Centeno realized he still didn't know what he was looking for. He could see the sign once Feltner pointed it out, but until then, it just didn't exist in his eyes.

When the spotlight ran across the tracks inside the fence, Feltner hit the brakes. He backed the vehicle up to bring the sign into view again and got out for a good look. "Seems they milled around some before decidin' not to cross," he said to Centeno, who had come around to look.

"Fresh?" Centeno asked.

"Oh yeah, these boys are definitely catchable."

"It's surprising you could see them."

"Naw, this is good cuttin'," Feltner demurred. "Ground like this, once you got your eye trained, you can track a piss ant in the moonlight." He took out his small notebook and ballpoint and started making more sketches. When he finished, he walked back to the vehicle to radio head-quarters. "Got the sign of four out here on the state high-way just south of Spofford. Looks like they could be the same four that sensors picked up down by the canal and the ranch road. Is Peters comin' out this way? Over." He lis-tened to the voice beneath the pop of static, then answered, "Okay. We'll get on 'em. Ten-four."

"Might as well cut up this fence line to the ranch road," he said to Centeno. "Cut west there, and we'll know if these boys are still in the pasture or somewheres else."

"Shhh," Javier stopped suddenly, and they all listened to the faint hum rising on the road to the south. It got louder and closer, then stopped as if the vehicle had turned off. The sky had washed out to a pale gray, and the lighter it got, the more anxious Javier became. The ground was al-most perfectly flat, the mesquite was thin, and they had yet to see a good place to hide. From the air, Javier was sure they could be easily spotted. When the noise didn't resume, they continued through the mesquite.

They had walked perhaps another fifty yards when they heard the sound of a vehicle. This time, however, it didn't sound as if it were on the highway but coming slowly through the brush behind them. The four veered sharply away from the road until Juan, the last in line, stopped. "Look!" he said and pointed at the headlights moving slowly through the mesquite along the fence line, a spotlight tracking inside the fence. Automatically, they dropped to the ground.

"What are they doing?"

"Looking for our tracks." Javier stood to watch the vehicle until it passed. "Let's go," he said and started back in the direction they had just come from.

Full light was upon them as they trotted toward the highway. Ten yards out from the fence, Javier came to an abrupt halt. Before him in the light, he could see where the strips on both sides of the fence had been cleared and brushed out. Looking at the others meaningfully, he clinched his molars in a grimace. "Farther back, we walked in this. They already know we're here."

Circling back, they made a loop through the brush that brought them to the highway at a point farther south. Javier stopped at the cleared strip and turned his back to it. "Walk backward," he told the others, "and maybe we'll confuse them." They all turned their backs, backed across the clearing, climbed the fence, and backed to the highway. On pavement where their tracks would come to a temporary halt, they ran south for as long as they dared before crossing into the pasture.

Feltner switched off the headlights when the sun was completely up, and Centeno tried watching the ground just below his window. The rapid passage of small rocks quickly made his eyes tired and his stomach queasy. Twice they stopped to examine a sign, but both times Feltner dismissed it as being something other than the four they were after. They had just turned onto the ranch road west when Peters pulled off the highway and stopped his vehicle next to theirs. Brown hair, a trimmed mustache, and brown eyes, he had the high gloss that comes with overfeeding. Unlike the other PIs, who wore cowboy hats, he had on the official Smokey the Bear hat issued by the Border Patrol. "Lose something?" he asked sarcastically.

Feltner smiled. "Here's what we got." He took out his pad. "Walking shoe with a half moon sittin' cockeyed in the heel, cowboy boot, round-toe boot, and another cowboy boot with a diamond-shaped plug in the heel." He handed the pad to Centeno, and Centeno passed it through the window to Peters.

Peters studied the pad a minute, took out a ballpoint, and copied the different tracks on his palm and the inside of his wrist. "Which way?"

"Why don't you cut this fence west along the ranch road to see if they've already jumped out. We'll go back to where we first picked up their sign."

"Whatever you say, boss." Peters drove away; Feltner and

Centeno pulled in their tire, turned around, and drove south on the highway. Beyond where he recalled seeing the sign, Feltner turned off the highway and started north again along the fence. When he saw the tracks, he stopped the vehicle and they got out. He studied the tracks a minute, walked to the back of their Dodge Ramcharger, peed, and came back to his open door. After attaching a walkie-talkie to his belt, he pulled out a bag of Red Man tobacco. "Chew?" he invited and held the package toward Centeno. Centeno said, "no, thanks," but watched as Feltner rolled a small ball of loose tobacco leaves and inserted it in his left cheek. "Guess we're ready," Feltner said cheerfully, and they climbed the fence.

"How'd you happen to get into this?" Feltner asked as they followed the clear tracks on the brushed-out lane.

"Oh I don't know," Centeno said vaguely. "Finished junior college and the career counselor suggested the Border Patrol since I knew Spanish. At first I thought it would be against *la raza*, you know, but then I figured somebody had to do it." He turned to Feltner. "What about you?"

"Went broke," Feltner said. "Tried windmillin', ranchin', truckin', you name it. Finally, my wife came into some money when her daddy died, so we decided to get in the truckin' business for ourselves. Both trucks, nice diesels, were sittin' together when a flash flood hit. Wiped us clean out."

"Didn't you have insurance?"

"Had insurance for everything but floods. Didn't think it was necessary in West Texas."

"That's too bad."

"Act of God," Feltner squirted a stream of tobacco juice. "Anyways, that's when a friend who was in suggested I join the Patrol. I was ready for a little security by that time, and nobody else was gonna pay me to play cowboys and Indians."

The tracks cut away from the lane, and they walked more slowly through the mesquite. On the harder crust of soil, all Centeno could see was an occasional scuffed place and, sometimes when Feltner stopped to examine them, bent weeds. It was rare when they came across anything that looked vaguely like a footprint. They hadn't gone far when the walkie-talkie began to squawk and they could hear Peters' voice. "I've cut this fence line all the way to the bend where the road turns south. No sign. Over."

Feltner raised his walkie-talkie. "We're on their trail about thirty yards in from the fence. Why don't you come back this way and start walking us a line from the other end? Over."

"Parallel to the fence? Over."

"That's right. Thirty, forty yards in."

"Fine with me," Peters said and signed off.

"I'll bet you these ol' boys bushed up somewhere along here and went sound to sleep," Feltner said to Centeno as they started walking. They moved through the brush at an uneven yet deliberate pace until Feltner stopped and pointed out an area where the weeds were pressed flat. "Looks like they took a little nap," he said and started walking again. He hadn't gone but a few steps when he came to another halt and bent to search the ground more closely. "Goddog, what'd they do now?" Slowly, crouched down with his hands on his knees, he backed to the place where the weeds were flattened, then made a slow circle till he came to the tracks pointing south. "Well, that beats the dickens," he stood up straight and tipped his hat back.

"What's that?" Centeno asked.

"They switched directions, heading south. Ain't likely they decided to go home." He looked around carefully till he noticed the view of the highway. "Now I got it. These boys seen us driving along the fence line, hid in the grass here, then backtracked. Sure enough, that's what they did." He pulled out his walkie-talkie to advise Peters to go back to his vehicle and meet them on the state highway, then turned and started following the sign.

They followed the tracks to the lane, then walked the big loop the Mexicans had made back toward the highway. "Now look at this," Feltner said when they came to the lane the second time.

Centeno studied the ground. "This is where they came into the pasture?" he asked doubtfully, looking at the tracks that appeared to come from the highway.

"That's sure what they'd like for us to think," Feltner said. "But look again. See how short the stride is here. And look how the toe is deeper than the heelprint. Man walking normal puts more weight on his heel."

"Then they backed across here."

"That's right. Look close," he was standing at the edge of the lane, "and you can see where they turned in their tracks."

"Pretty tricky," Jessie admired.

"And it might of worked too, had we just been cuttin'

from a vehicle. That's why you got to walk sign. Walkin', goin' from one track to the next, the sign always has got to make sense. And there's hardly no way to get across ground without leavin' sign. Look close enough and you see it. Yes, sir, Jessie, it's always there."

They climbed the fence and crossed to the highway. "Here it gets difficult," Feltner said. "Since they aren't gonna leave any sign on the pavement, we have to go down and pick it up again along this fence line. Likely we'll find it."

From the highway to the fence, Armando led the way, with the others stepping in his footsteps and Javier coming last, brushing out the individual tracks with a mesquite branch. They climbed the fence, negotiated the lane within, and bolted through the mesquite away from the road. They ran until out of breath and well out of sight. "*Miran*," Javier said, panting, "here we slow them down. Fan out in the brush but stay close enough not to get lost. They'll have to follow four trails." So dispersed, they turned north again and moved through the brush parallel with the highway. They walked for perhaps thirty minutes before approaching another dirt road and fence line. Javier hissed at the others and signaled not to cross. Instead, they turned east into the hot morning sun until they came to railroad tracks that ran north to Spofford.

"Step on the rails and ties," Javier said to the others, "and you won't leave a trail. You two run that way, and Juan and

I will go this way. If they get an airplane, it will be harder for them to see two than four."

Stepping from tie to tie, Armando and Toño ran until looking back they saw that Javier and Juan had disappeared from the roadbed.

Heads down, Feltner and Centeno were walking slowly along the highway when Peters drove up. "What happened?" Peters asked.

"They backtracked on us," Feltner said. "We cut their sign coming across the highway. Now we're trying to pick it up on this side."

"You want a hand?"

"I'd prefer an airplane. Why don't you see if headquarters can give us an aerial assist. Then, if you want, go on up the highway and see if there's a gap in this fence. Seems like there's one where you can get in and cut a line north of here."

Peters drove off, and Feltner and Centeno continued along the fence. The ground was hard white caliche that had been scraped clean except for occasional white pebbles. Centeno didn't see how a footstep could mark the ground. He lost hope of seeing sign, lost energy, and began to think about how hot it was getting. No longer really looking, he walked along behind Feltner, who moved in a near trance-like state of concentration. After 150 yards, Feltner stopped at a fence post and pointed to a small scuff mark. "Can't get over a fence without leaving some sort of sign," he said and walked away from the post toward the highway.

Fifteen yards out, he turned and squatted down to look at the ground as if across a pool table. "Pretty smart," he said. "Yes, sir, Jessie, this is a smart one. Most wets, when they want to brush out their tracks, brush out too much and leave a trail behind them you can see for miles. This one just brushed out the individual footsteps. You can see it but not so easy."

They crossed the fence and followed the running footsteps without any problem until the footsteps turned north and fanned out. Feltner followed the first trail, then made a slow zigzag across the pasture to pick up the other three. When he had the fourth trail, he pulled out his walkie-talkie. "Peters, you find that gap? I've got four different trails headin' north. Over." He waited a minute, then repeated the message.

"Got you," Peters came on. "I was just closin' the fence. I'm on a road that will cut east in front of you. Over."

"What about that plane?"

"It's on the way. Over."

Slowly Feltner moved north, following first one trail, then another, keeping the four in hand like reins to a team of horses. Through the mesquite, they caught sight of Peters' vehicle crawling across the pasture along the fence, then disappear into the mesquite. Just as Feltner and Centeno got to the fence and the junction of the four trails, they heard the rapid, four-wheel whine and saw Peters coming back toward them. He stopped at the fence and hung out the window. "Didn't cross this road," he called.

"We got their sign here," Feltner called back. "They're peelin' off to the sun again. What's up there, anyways?"

"Railroad. Branch of the Southern Pacific that runs into Spofford."

"Can you get past it in your vehicle?"

"No problem."

"Well, go up and see if you can cut back south—head these boys off."

Feltner and Centeno followed where the tracks cut east, then veered back into the mesquite away from the fence. Above, the sky had turned a dull white with the morning heat; the dark green shirts of their uniforms had begun to turn black with perspiration. "Wish that goddog plane would get here," Feltner glanced up at the sky with annoyance.

At the railroad tracks, they stopped and looked north, then south. "Here's where it gets tough," Feltner said. "Like at the highway, they're gonna have run one direction or the other on the ties to spread out their sign. Might as well check south first; that's what they've favored so far."

Peering carefully at the ground, they moved along the roadbed, where the heat seemed greater for the smell of creosote kindled in the ties. After a hundred yards, they turned, walked quickly to where they began, and started north. Feltner had no doubt they would cut the sign; the ground next to the gravelbed was knee-deep with weeds and a thin, sandy crust beyond. It was only a matter of time.

In the west, they heard the distant hum of a small plane. "Hope that's for us," Feltner said without looking up. "Sure would be nice to have a plane fly over to get these boys to bush up. Save us some walkin'."

The plane passed high, circled, and came skimming across

the tops of the trees at them, washing them in a wake of noise and wind. "Who is that?" Feltner said into his walkie-talkie, looking up at the frail, green-and-white Piper Cub.

"Lett," a staticky voice answered. "What you got down there?"

"Four brush walkers somewhere east of these railroad tracks. I'm fixin' to cut their sign. Till I do, buzz the area to hold 'em down."

"Sure thing," the voice cracked.

"Hey, you see Peters?"

"He's cutting a dirt road. Parallels the tracks about a quarter mile east."

"Good enough," Feltner signed off.

The plane made a sharp, slow turn behind them that brought the engine to a near stall, then flew back overhead toward Peters. Beyond Peters, it cut another turn and was coming back when Feltner noticed the trampled weeds. "I've got their sign," he called into his walkie-talkie and waved at Lett. "Fly us a line!" Lett wagged the plane's wings in response. "Peters," Feltner barked. "You hear us?"

"Yeah."

"Lett's gonna fly us a line. Get on it at that end."

Feltner started into the mesquite, with Centeno close behind. "Yes, sir, Jesús," Feltner said with excitement, "now we're in business."

The plane turned behind them, then swooped back just above the path they walked, riveting the brush with its engine noise. Beyond Peters it turned again, came back, and made another pass above Feltner. Midway, they heard Lett shout, "Got 'em! Feltner, they're straight ahead of you and Centeno."

"Let's go," Feltner shouted and broke into a run. The plane skidded off its course, circled back, and went into a slow, sickening turn that kept it at a near stall above a dense clump of mesquite.

Feltner and Centeno ran hard weaving through the brush until a patch of maroon and the form of a body buried under leaves caught Feltner's eye. "*Somos de la inmigración*," he shouted into the thicket.

Dry, fernlike mesquite leaves fell away as Toño, then Armando sat up. Both looked embarrassed—inadequate to all the fuss.

Peters came running up; the Piper Cub broke out of its turn to circle wide. "*¿Donde están los otros?*" Feltner demanded.

Toño and Armando shrugged their shoulders and began to slowly brush the leaves and dirt from their clothes.

"Centeno, you check the soles of their shoes to see which ones we got." Feltner took up the walkie-talkie. Peters was already circling the thicket looking for the others. "Lett," Feltner called into the radio, "we got two."

"You think y'all can find the others?" Lett asked through the static. "I'm about out of fuel. Been up here since daylight."

"We'll find 'em."

"Okay. Over." The sound of the engine began to fade.

"We've got the walking shoe with a half moon and a plain cowboy boot," Centeno reported. "That leaves the round-toe boot and the diamond-plug cowboy boot."

"Feltner," Peters walked up from the direction of the railroad tracks, "I only see the sign of two coming in here. Did you have four?"

"Didn't have time to count." Then, to Armando and Toño, "*¿Verdad, donde están los otros?*"

"*¿Quién sabe?*" Toño answered.

Javier and Juan listened as the plane droned away toward Eagle Pass. They had, as Feltner suspected, started south on the railroad tracks, but in a last moment of inspiration, jumped off to the west and headed back toward the highway. From a thick clump of mesquite, they had watched as the plane circled and surmised that Toño and Armando had been caught.

Stray voices came through the brush, then the solid quiet of searching. Javier and Juan listened tensely until they heard Peters' vehicle start and drive back to the highway where Feltner had left his. Feltner's vehicle started and both drove away.

"*Ay, los pobres*," Javier said sadly of Armando and Toño.

"*Sí*," Juan agreed. "*Y tienen la comida y agua.*" Yes, and they have the food and water.

Javier and Juan fell asleep where they were. They slept the rest of the day and didn't move until evening came on and the level of their hunger and thirst approached that of their fatigue. Thinking that at least they would find water, they started walking. The sun setting behind them, and after an interim of dark, the moon rising before, they walked with the simple desire to keep going.

The terrain gradually began to change from the mesquite flats to rough, gully-cut ground. Not thinking the gullies might be dry branches of a creek, they trudged on till Javier pointed to a dark line of trees that stood out against the sky. At the bottom of a bank beneath the cottonwoods lay a string of small pools. They climbed down the bank, knelt before the water, and cupped it to their mouths.

That night they walked until the moon was low in the west, then slept till the sun woke them. In the morning they drank at another creek. At the side of a paved road, they picked up beer bottles to carry water the next time they found it. After two days without eating, they shambled on as if nothing in the landscape were more real or immediate than the black dots that would swarm before their eyes. Juan carried a rock, and each time a rabbit popped up, he would throw listlessly, saying, *"Vente conejo. Te quiero comer."* Come rabbit. I want to eat you.

By midmorning they had begun to look for a shady spot to sleep when they saw white boxes scattered in the brush. Proportioned like small apartment buildings, the boxes had flat roofs and a closed, sinister look. "What could those be?" Javier wondered aloud.

"Hive boxes," Juan answered. "For bees."

"Ah," Javier said with no interest and without stopping. He walked on until he realized he had left Juan behind, feverishly searching the ground. "What happened?" Javier said and looked at Juan. "What are you looking for?"

"There's honey in those boxes."

"There are also bees that will sting you to death if you bother them."

"Maybe," Juan said, picking up a stick and discarding it. "And maybe they're tame." He found a foot-long stick with a sharp point and tested its strength on his knee. His behavior was suddenly animated, and his eyes looked crafty.

"What if they sting you?"

"It won't kill me. Grandfather gets bees to sting him when he has arthritis."

"But not a whole hive."

"If they're mean," Juan said, "I'll run."

Armed with his stick, Juan approached one of the boxes. At the base in front, a protruding board was acrawl with bees landing and taking off. Circling to the back, Juan could hear the muted buzz of life within. He cautiously lifted the top off the box so that the buzzing sprang up in volume and pitch to a hectic reverberation. Bees crawled in and out and over the tops of the wooden frames that filled the box like files in a cabinet. Slowly Juan inserted the stick beneath the top of a frame and pried one end up. He pried the other end, grasped the frame in the middle and pulled, revealing a slice of comb alive with crawling bees. The bees continued to crawl over the comb, crawled over Juan's hand, but didn't fly or seem to notice the disturbance. Juan gently brushed the bees off his hand with the stick and scraped the length of the stick across the cone to nudge the bees back into the box. After he had pulled another frame, he closed the box and carried the rectangles of honeycomb to Javier.

"Very good," Javier smiled, impressed.

"Do we eat it here?" Juan handed Javier one of the frames.

Javier held the cone up to the sunlight. In some of the open cells he could see the brown glisten of honey, but most were capped with wax to protect either the honey or the larvae within. "Let's look for shade," he said.

They walked till they came to a scrub oak and sat down. Juan broke off a piece of comb from the end of the frame, put it in his mouth, and bit down, exploding the sweet against his tongue. "Rich," he gasped. The honey, combined with heat, hunger, and thirst, sent a convulsive shudder through his stomach.

"Pure energy." Javier took a small bite and made a face. He chewed the comb, then took the wad of wax from his mouth and looked at it. "We should save this. It might be useful."

"Too bad we don't have bread," Juan licked his fingers. "This will make us sick before it fills us."

"Or at least water."

Juan considered the cells with larvae. "Perhaps the babies are good to eat."

"If they are, tell me," Javier answered.

After they had eaten as much as they could stomach, they hung the frames on a branch of the tree and went to sleep. They woke late in the afternoon, ate more of the honey, and started walking, carrying what was left of the combs.

When they came to a windmill, they drank, took off their shirts to rinse them out, and washed their hands, faces, and torsos. They sat beneath the windmill listening to its uneven creak and watched the sun swell red on the clear horizon.

Javier sighed deeply several times. "We need to walk," he finally said. The sun sank, the sky turned pale, Venus shone white. Javier stood up, then Juan. They put on their cold, wet shirts, washed out and filled the beer bottles, and started.

They made their way through the dark until the waning moon rose before them. The land turned ridgy; the brush grew thick. Late in the night, they came to a fence. The fence stood eight feet tall; its posts were made of concrete and bent outward at the top so that from the ground, Javier and Juan looked straight up at four strands of barbed wire that projected over their heads. "Someone doesn't want us to come in," Javier said.

"Which way?" Juan asked. "North or south?"

"North." They followed the fence through the night until toward dawn they saw the rapid passage of headlights along a highway. They crossed the highway and railroad tracks that ran parallel, moved out of sight into the brush, and started east again. When the sun came up, the traffic on the highway increased and they occasionally caught sight of cars and trucks through gaps in the mesquite. A train whistle blew, and they stopped to listen to the slow passage. "San Antonio," Javier said when it was gone.

At a small tin shed partially filled with baled alfalfa, they stopped to drink at a trough, then climbed onto the alfalfa and went to sleep. Heat radiating through the tin roof woke them early in the afternoon, and they got down to drink again. Javier broke off honeycomb from the frame he'd hung from a rafter, took a bite, and walked over to a cardboard barrel in the back of the shed. Inside he found large brown pellets of cow feed. He sniffed one of the pellets, rubbed honey on it, and put it in his mouth. He chewed slowly, letting the pellet dissolve, then swallowed. "Juan, I've found something we can eat," he said, his teeth brown with the feed.

They both ate the feed and honey, drank more water, and went back to sleep in the shade next to the shed.

When the heat let up, they started to walk again. They had to cross the highway when it turned north, but they continued just out of sight of the railroad. Their shadows stretched out ahead of them as they walked. They crossed a creek where they drank and passed a train sitting silent on a siding. Shadows dissolved slowly into the evening dark; large cumulus clouds glowed white with the last light of the day. Javier kept due east, focusing on red antennae lights in the distance until they heard the train coming slowly up the tracks from behind. They veered to the edge of the mesquite, watched the single eye of the dark locomotive approach and pass, and the slow procession of open wagons filled with asphalt. Javier and Juan looked at one another, dropped the frames of honey, and ran for the train.

Part V

THE SURFACE OF tar began to shine as heat transformed it from a solid to a liquid. "*Está caliente*," Juan said, watching a black bubble break the surface.

"Four hundred fifty degrees," Ascensión shouted from the temperature gauge at the end of the tar kettle, "Five, and it will be ready." As he stood on his toes to look in at the tar, his long nose above the trim mustache and the mobile eyebrows gave him an inquisitive air. Sixty-three years old, Ascensión looked fit, if not dapper, in the gray uniform and white hardhat.

The heat made the sides of the vat appear to sweat tar, and the air filled with the smell. Beneath the vat, the pressurized kerosene burners roared like small jet engines. Ascensión gave the pressure tank for the kerosene a few swift pumps, then signaled for Juan to follow. Above, on top of the house, the rest of the crew was preparing the roof for the hot tar. Ascensión unhooked a long metal pipe from the side of the trailer and, with Juan's help, extended one end up over the edge of the roof and connected the other to a gasoline pump at the end of the vat.

"See this," Ascensión indicated a rope attached loosely to both ends of the pipe. "When you're up on the roof, you pull that end of the rope and it will pull this lever to the pump." He tied the rope to the lever. "Pull the rope and tar comes out of the pipe. Let go and it stops. Very simple."

Juan nodded his understanding and inserted a finger to scratch beneath his hardhat. They hadn't started working, but his hair was soaked with perspiration.

"Over here," Ascensión led the way, "we have the *chapapote*." Ninety-pound bulks of tar lay stacked on the ground. Cylindrical, they were wrapped in brown paper like huge pieces of taffy. Ascensión rolled one of the cylinders to the tar vat, slit the paper down the side with a knife, and lifted it up to shoulder height to lower it into the smoking vat. They watched it sink and begin to melt like a cube of ice. "Put in five," Ascensión said, holding up five fingers in his heavy gloves before taking them off and handing them to Juan. Juan took the gloves and started for the *chapapote*. "Julio," Ascensión called Juan back, "when you put the *chapapote* in," he rolled up his sleeve, "don't drop it!" He held out the inside of his forearm to show Juan a topographic map of white scar tissue. "It's very hot," Ascensión smiled with meaning.

Juan grimaced and started back toward the *chapapote*. Late the preceding afternoon, he had become Julio when Javier came in from work with a pale-blue, laminated card that said Julio Sáenz and gave a place of birth, date, and, most important, a Social Security number. The card was forged but the Social Security number was authentic, so that an account existed for Juan's earnings. "At work, call yourself Julio," Javier had told him. "I'm Francisco or Frank. I'm not your brother. Don't forget and call me Javier."

They had been in San Antonio three days, had arrived at sunup Sunday morning. Javier had gone back to work Monday. By Tuesday, he had arranged the Social Security number and a job for Juan. He had also stopped talking.

Juan put on the gloves and rolled one of the cylinders of tar to the vat. At 130 pounds, Juan wasn't much heavier than his load. He cut off the paper, got a firm grip, and heaved the cylinder to the edge of the vat. Slowly he lowered the opposite end before letting go and jumping back. The cylinder slid in with a minimal splash. Juan stepped forward to watch it settle next to the other cylinder. Through the smoke rising about the tar, he could see Javier and another man on the roof talking and laughing.

When Juan finished, Ascensión told him to go up on the roof and help clean up. A machine similar to a lawn mower had been used the day before to tear off the old gravel and tar. Most of it had been shoveled up and carried off, but the roof had to be swept clean before new rolls of asphalt paper could be put down. As he pushed a broom, Juan watched Javier, who was measuring, then cutting pieces of new lumber with an electric saw. He wore a carpenter's belt and was in charge of replacing old gravel guards, flashings, and parts of the roof where the boards beneath were rotten. Juan pushed several piles of gravel and scraps together, scooped them up in a large shovel, and dropped them into the dump truck that had been backed up to the edge of the house. It was hot on the roof; the sky above San Antonio was a glaring, carbon-monoxide gray. Below, the racket of the pump's gasoline engine joined the roar of the kerosene burners. Juan watched an American come out of the house next door, get into a brown sports car, and drive away. In every direction he could see flat gravel roofs like the one he stood on.

"Julio!" Ascensión poked his head over the edge of the roof. "Come with me," he said and disappeared. Juan climbed down the ladder and followed Ascensión to the pickup where he was hacking dried tar and gravel off the wheels of a small hand truck with a hatchet. When the wheels were clean, he turned the truck over and placed a large metal drum within the metal bands that held it to the truck. "Take this up on the roof," Ascensión directed. Juan rolled the hand truck to the ladder and dragged it up behind him. Ascensión followed with a large mop and a five-gallon bucket. "Ready?" Ascensión called to the foreman and his assistant.

"Ready," they called back. Both the foreman and his assistant were large men made larger by their heavy, thick-soled boots and hardhats. Enormous muttonchop sideburns and a mustache gave the foreman a fierce look.

Ascensión and Juan rolled the tub to the pipe that was connected to the vat of tar, positioned the tub beneath, and pulled the rope. The tar that gushed out was preceded by and enveloped in smoke so that the tub appeared to be filling with nothing more than hot vapor. When it approached the rim, the black liquid came into view, and Ascensión let go of the rope. He rolled the tub to the far end of the roof and gave the foreman the mop. While his assistant brought a large roll of black paper from the front of the roof, the foreman dipped the mop in the tub as if testing the tar.

"*Mira*," Ascensión explained to Juan, "when they want more tar, fill this bucket," he held up the five-gallon bucket. "Take it and pour it into the tub. When they want paper, get paper. Don't get in the way of the mop and don't spill tar on yourself." Juan nodded earnestly, pulled on his heavy gloves, and waited by the pipe. The foreman lifted the heavy, steaming mop out of the tub and made a fast sweep at the edge of the roof, leaving three main pools of boiling tar and spreading a cloud of smoke through the air. When his assistant rolled the asphalt paper over the tar, it sizzled through to the surface. Juan watched their progress until the foreman shouted "*¡Chapapote!*" then filled the bucket, grabbed its handle, and leaning away from the weight, staggered across the roof to pour the tar into the tub. "*¡Papel!*" the assistant shouted as soon as Juan had returned to the pipe. Juan rushed to the front of the house, swung a sixty-pound roll of asphalt paper onto his shoulder, and, stepping fast, carried it to the men.

The strips of asphalt rolled across the roof, the black surface collecting the heat, the pools of hot tar glittering in the sun. Not talking, sweating through the gray uniforms, the men moved within a cloud of smoke. Javier, Juan realized, was watching him. But each time Juan looked in his direction, Javier looked away. Since they had gotten out of the car that morning, Javier had shown no sign that he knew Juan.

When they had covered the roof with one layer of the paper, they started again, overlapping the rolls to build up three layers. Juan's knees began to shake as he went from paper to tar, and a continuous stream of sweat poured out of his hardhat into his eyes. Other than the heat radiating against his right leg when he carried the bucket, the potentially dangerous slap of the mop, and the weight of the rolls of asphalt, Juan was aware of nothing but *"¡Chapapote! ¡Papel!"*

After the last roll of paper, they broke for lunch. Juan climbed down the ladder at the front of the house, stopped for a drink of water from the tar-splattered cup that was tied with a string to the water cooler, and fell supine in the shade to wait for Javier. Ascensión had already gotten his black metal lunch box and was carefully peeling a cucumber. Moving the tip of his tongue in conjunction with the blade of his pocketknife, Ascensión sliced away the rind except for a cap of green at the bottom to hold on to. From the top, he quartered the cucumber, then spread the sections with his fingers to salt the pulpy center, closed his eyes, and took a bite.

Javier walked up from the truck with the lunch kit, dropped a foil package next to Juan, and, without a word, walked off and sat down alone. Bewildered, Juan looked at him, then slowly opened the package of tacos. He ate and lay back down with his hardhat over his face. When he woke, the men were already on the roof, and he had the sad feeling of not knowing where he was.

The afternoon went like the morning except that they covered the tar with gravel rather than asphalt paper. A large conveyor belt carried the gravel from a dump truck to wheelbarrows on the roof. Javier and another man pushed the wheelbarrows to where the foreman spread the tar that Juan brought in buckets while his assistant shoveled. By the time they had finished and packed up all the equipment, it was after five. Juan rode in the pickup with Ascensión. Back at company headquarters, he saw Javier go up onto the loading dock and into the room where the crews congregated in the morning. Juan considered following but decided to wait in the car. He walked out to the parking lot, climbed into the old blue Pontiac, and slumped down to rest. The paint on the car was dead, the fenders dented, its upholstery ripped and torn, but as far as Juan knew, it was the first car anyone in the family had owned. And Javier was the first to learn how to drive.

Javier dropped his lunch box and hardhat through the window into the back seat and got in. He didn't speak but he started the car and they drove slowly, springs squeaking, through the affluent neighborhoods of North San Antonio to the downtown section, where the streets looked empty and stale in the afternoon glare. West on Commerce Street, they went past the old Farmers' Market, beneath the expressway, and into West San Antonio. They turned off the main thoroughfare, drove through a freshly paved parking lot, and stopped the car in front of a small frame shack that looked across an alley into the lot. "I'm going to buy food," Javier said and waited for Juan to get out.

Juan let himself in the chain-link fence, crossed the caliche strip of yard, and unlocked the door on a dark room, dense with stored heat. He switched on the overhead light, stuck his hand behind the red curtain and venetian blinds to raise the front window, and went into the kitchen to open the back door. In the front room, he took the exposed copper ends of a fan's electric cord and shoved them into a wall socket. The fan, a salvaged remnant from an evaporative cooler, tapped its metal frame on each slow rotation to evolve a constant metallic clang and a slight breeze. Exhausted and hot, he lay down on the warm, lumpy bed and stared first at the pink ceiling, then at a framed picture on the wall of a red-lipped woman playing a guitar.

When Javier came in, he took a bag of groceries in to the small table in the kitchen. He pulled loose the strip of black electrical tape that held the refrigerator door closed, emptied the pan of rusty water that dripped out of the small freezing compartment, and stored the food. Walking into the front room, he took off his shirt then pants and hung them along with his other clothes on nails driven into the wall. In the bathroom, avoiding the rotten floorboards beneath the worn linoleum rug, he edged past the toilet and lavatory to climb into the moldy shower stall that doubled as storage for a mop and rags. He turned on warm water to lather and scrub himself with a knot of sisal, then cold to try to cool off. As he dried off, sweat broke out on his skin so that he was still wet when he put on underwear that he kept stored in the gutted stereo cabinet in the front room.

Through the front door, he could tell by the slant of light on the parking lot that the sun was going down, and above, the tin roof popped hollowly as the trapped heat diminished. He snapped on the radio—part of a plastic phonograph set—to the local Spanish station, pulled on clean pants and platform shoes, and went into the kitchen.

Juan managed to drag himself off the bed. On the way to the bathroom, he noticed that Javier was spooning gray lard from a jar into a skillet on the stove. A cold pot of boiled potatoes sat on the table among the dirty dishes that had been there since morning. When Juan came out, Javier was tearing the skin off the potatoes with his fingernails. Onions were simmering in the lard. Juan dressed, took the plate of potatoes and onions scrambled with eggs and the glass of punch Javier put out, and ate standing by the door. When he finished, Juan put his empty plate in the kitchen sink, ran water over a rag dipped in detergent, and began to wash the few plastic plates and glasses. Shirtless beneath the raw light bulb, Javier was rolling out tortillas with a glass on the tabletop; perspiration dripped from his face into the white flour.

Juan finished the dishes, and went to lie on his edge of the bed. Beneath the blare of the radio, he could hear the thump of a jukebox from across the parking lot, and, staring at the floor, could see beneath the crust of dirt to the original pattern of green-and-yellow spots that decorated the cracked and peeling linoleum.

The alarm clock went off, and Juan could hear Javier get up and go in the dark into the bathroom. The toilet flushed, then the light snapped on in the ceiling. Juan squinted at Javier. "What's wrong? What time is it?"

"Five," Javier said and pulled on the gray trousers to his uniform.

"Five? Already?"

"Get up. We have to make breakfast, then lunch." Javier pulled on his shirt and went into the kitchen.

The week passed. Each morning they got up at five to prepare food and eat, went to work at seven, and came home at night in time to eat again, bathe, and sleep for the next day. Javier continued to ignore Juan and didn't speak unless it was necessary. On Friday, Juan learned that the crew worked on Saturdays. On Saturday, Javier told him they were going to work for an independent shingle contractor on Sunday. It was an unrelieved existence of work, heat, and exhaustion.

By Monday, Juan had begun to drag. Javier's silence wore at him, and he saw no point to the hard work if there was no prospect of pleasure or at least rest. Resenting Javier, resenting each call for tar or paper, he didn't realize his feelings showed until Tuesday at lunch. "Keep acting the way you are," Javier said as he handed Juan his tacos, "and they'll run you off." That afternoon Juan saw that the foreman was watching him. The suspicion hurt his feelings, then made him belligerent. "Let them fire me," he would say to himself. "I don't care."

Javier disappeared on Tuesday night. He bathed, put on a good shirt and trousers, combed his hair carefully, and left in the car. Thinking Javier would come back and never having cooked, Juan waited to eat until hunger coerced him into making bread and margarine sandwiches. He took the sandwiches and a glass of punch to sit on the step in front of the house where he listened to the mournful thump of the jukebox rise and fall each time someone opened the door to La Segunda Cumbia de Paco. In the distance, two red lights tracked up and down the side of a tower topped by a saucer-shaped platform. The platform, Juan noticed, was slowly rotating. It looked strange and made him see how far away from home he was. He thought of his parents and decided to leave as soon as he was paid.

Juan woke when Javier came in, but neither of them spoke. Juan felt better the next day and worked harder. The end was in sight.

Thursday night, Javier again left without explanation. Juan ate, gathered up the pennies on top of the old stereo cabinet, and walked to La Segunda Cumbia to buy a quart of beer. He brought the beer back to the house, where he sat on the front step and watched the tower platform revolve. While he drank, he pondered Javier's meanness. He finished the beer, and, slightly high, went for another. Sitting on the steps again, he began to think of his mother, then thought of his girlfriend. "Ay, Lourdes!" he said when, for the first time, he remembered that he hadn't said good-bye. He went inside to turn on the radio, a song ended, and after an announcement, a man began singing "El Huerfanito." Juan listened to the maudlin song about the little orphan and thought of how he had left poor little Lourdes all alone and had barely thought of her. The skin on his cheeks grew tight, the tears ran down his face, and he could taste the salt at the back of his throat easing the lump. "Poor little Lourdes," he kept saying to himself and finally took a black crayon, made a large cross on the wall above his pillow, and wrote her name in bold letters. He put his head on the pillow and felt better until he thought of Leti, then got up and wrote her name on the wall next to Lourdes'. He finished the beer and lay back down to think of poor Lourdes and poor Leti. When he woke, he didn't know if it was night or morning, whether Javier was getting up or going to bed.

"What have you been doing?" Javier stood over the bed, glaring at him. "You've gotten drunk. Written on the walls. Acted just as I knew you would."

Juan scowled at Javier, then turned his face to the wall. The skin around his eyes burned from the tears, and he could still taste the salt.

"What's wrong with you?" Javier said and took off his shirt. "Do you know how easy you have it? I got you a job, I take you to work, I feed you." Javier kicked off his shoes. "You have a place to live. What do you want? When I came, I had nothing. No one helped me, I had to rent a room every day, and if I couldn't find work for the day, I didn't have a place to sleep or anything to eat." He stood and stared down at Juan's back. "Why don't you grow up and stop being such a baby?"

Juan lay tense, his face to the wall, and refused to answer. "I shouldn't have brought you," Javier said in a quieter voice. "I'm too young to raise you."

Juan rolled over and looked at him. "Don't worry. I'm leaving," he said and turned back to the wall.

The next morning when they left for work, Javier took a pillow from the bed and put it in the car. They didn't speak, but Juan's attitude made it clear that he was still angry. At lunch, Javier gave Juan the carne guizada and tortillas he had prepared and sat down on the grass next to him. "Hot, isn't it?" he said.

"Yes, it's hot," Juan said and got up to get a drink of water.

After work when Javier went out to the car, he saw Juan slumped down on the front seat. Rather than going to the driver's side, he walked around and opened Juan's door. "What?" Juan demanded and looked up belligerently, as if Javier might be telling him he couldn't have a ride. Javier reached in his pocket and held out the car keys. "You should probably learn how to drive," he said.

Juan looked at the keys. "Now?" he asked.

Javier turned down the corners of his mouth to make a serious face and nodded "Yes."

Juan reached for the keys. "Okay," he said, resisting the urge to smile.

Javier showed Juan how to move the seat up, gave him the pillow to sit on, and explained the fundamentals. Juan could barely see over the dashboard, his foot just reached the gas pedal, but when he turned the key, the engine started and he felt a surge of triumph. Sitting next to him, Javier demonstrated the automatic transmission and told him that when he steered he must focus on the front left fender to know where he was going. "It's the other fenders that are difficult," he warned.

They made slow circles in the parking lot, the car lurching to halts until Juan learned to step gently on the power brakes. After mastering a smooth start and stop, and securing a promise of more lessons, Juan surrendered the steering wheel to Javier. On the way home, Juan was unable to contain his enthusiasm. "Someday, maybe I can drive home," he said.

"Someday," Javier agreed.

That night, when Javier began to cook supper, Juan offered to help. "Can you make tortillas?" Javier asked.

Juan shook his head.

"I'll show you. It's not hard." Javier got a bowl, mixed flour and water, and worked the dough to the proper consistency. "Make a little ball," he said, "and once it's round, roll it out with a glass." He dusted the tabletop with flour and rolled out the tortilla. Juan watched him make two, then gave it a try. After he had the process, he began to talk, asking about cars, how much they cost, whether Javier could take his car to Mexico, and on. As soon as Juan ate and did the supper dishes, he went out and sat in the car to practice for a few minutes before bed.

That weekend, they worked for the company on Saturday and for the independent contractor on Sunday. The contractor, like Juan and Javier, was employed at the roofing company the rest of the week. He only took jobs that could be completed on Sunday with the hope of someday building enough business to go on his own. Javier and Juan didn't earn as much with the contractor as with the company, where they made $3.75 and $2.65 per hour respectively, plus overtime, and they had to work harder and longer to finish the job in one day. Javier, however, said it was more money than they would make at home.

Juan was happy as long as he got to drive. Sunday night, Javier taught him to park the car in the narrow driveway next to their house without scraping the chain-link fence. While Javier took his shower, Juan backed the car in and out. He marveled that he could do it alone, and would stop only when Javier called him to help with supper.

Tuesday after work, Juan was sitting behind the steering wheel when Javier came out to the parking lot. "Not to-night," Javier said as he walked up to the driver's side. "I'm in a hurry."

Juan reluctantly moved over to the other side of the car. Javier got in and scooted the seat back. "You're going out tonight," Juan said.

"That's right." Javier started the car. "Do you want to come?"

"Where?"

"Come and see."

They bathed, changed, and drove back downtown, where Javier parked the car in a lot next to a large new building. The first floor was open courtyards and broad ramps. Juan followed Javier up one of the ramps, through glass doors, and into an air-conditioned lobby scattered with couches and chairs. Javier turned down the first corridor and kept going until Juan stopped to look through the small observa-tion window of a wooden door. "Hey!" he hissed, seeing rows of desks. "This is a school."

"That's right," Javier said, walking back for him. "It's not bad. Come on."

Juan pressed his back molars together as he'd seen Javier do to indicate distress, but followed along.

Students were sitting in the classroom when they walked in. Javier spoke to a couple of people and took a seat toward the back of the group. Juan sat down across the aisle from him. A pretty young Mexican girl with frizzy brown hair said "Hello" to Javier and gave Juan a look of appraisal. "Who's your friend?" she said to Javier.

"My brother," Javier answered.

She looked at Juan and grinned. "Going to learn English?" Juan scooted a notch lower in his desk and began to chew at a thumbnail. He jumped when the door at the back of the classroom slammed and a loud female voice rang through the room. The voice was incomprehensible, but everyone mumbled in response as the woman came walking up the aisle between Javier and Juan, her voice filling the room. A pale yellow dress brushed against Juan's desk as she passed, and he noticed black high heels, strong calves, and large hips. The woman set her books on the desk and turned. Still talking and smiling, her eyes were masked by large black-rimmed glasses that reflected the light.

The girl with the frizzy hair turned to smile surreptitiously at Juan, then looked back at the woman who, hands clasped before her, was striding deliberately toward Juan. She stopped before Juan's desk, her black high heels planted wide to support the body swaying gently from side to side. The voice rose in volume and pitch, then hung in waiting silence. She spoke again, more emphatically. One of the hands clasped before the stomach released itself and made a rotund gesture that ended palm up before Juan's face as if something might magically appear.

Juan forced himself to look up. No one had ever spoken English to him before; the only Anglos he had encountered were Border Patrolmen. The woman spoke again, directing the hand to herself, then to Juan. The hand waited. Juan tried to smile, shook his hair back over his collar, tried to catch his breath. Again she spoke, and the hand rotated to the girl with frizzy hair. The girl responded, and Juan understood the last word—Elena. The hand floated to Javier, and Juan heard the name Frank. When the open palm floated back before his face, Juan took a breath and ventured, "Julio."

"Repeat!" the woman said triumphantly. "My—name—is—Julio."

Juan managed to get the sentence out and repeated it until the woman was satisfied. When she turned away, he felt battered and exhausted. Javier tried to encourage him, but he was too nervous to pay attention and simply waited in fear that she would come back. When the class was over, he bolted. Javier found him sitting in the car.

"You didn't like it," Javier said as he got in. Juan shook his head and looked out his window. "Well, you don't have to go back."

On the way home, Javier stopped the car at a fried chicken franchise, went in, and came out with two boxes. They ate sitting in the car, watching through the plate-glass window as the young man in a red and white striped shirt waited on customers.

"That looks like good work," Juan remarked. "It wouldn't be so heavy."

"Probably not," Javier agreed.

"Put chicken in boxes, attend the customers, take the money." Juan watched with interest. "I could do all of that."

Javier dropped a bone into the box and wiped off his mouth with a napkin. "What would you say to the Anglos?"

Wednesday was payday. Javier stopped at a neighborhood grocery on the way home from work, had Juan endorse his check, and took both of their checks inside. When he came out, he gave Juan two ten-dollar bills.

"This is all?" Juan said as he fingered the bills.

"You made more," Javier started the car, "but we have expenses."

"Expenses?"

"Rent for two months. I got behind a month when I went to Jalisco. Two car payments—the same thing. And the store," he tilted his head back toward the grocery, "they've been selling us food on credit. Then we have to buy gas for the car. And I had to borrow a hundred dollars to go home. It adds up."

Juan looked down and rubbed the two bills together. "Then it's gone."

"This paycheck." Javier looked straight ahead. "Next time, maybe there will be more left over."

When they got to the house, Javier got out and let Juan scoot over to take the wheel. Juan parked the car in the driveway, then backed it out, made a loop through the parking lot, drove to the end of the alley, and backed up to the house. He started to park the car for the night, but on impulse drove to the end of the alley, out into the street, and circled the block.

Thursday night, Juan decided not to go to class with Javier. They worked that weekend. Sunday night, on the way home, they stopped at a traffic signal four blocks from their house. When the light turned green, Javier stepped on the accelerator and a distinct ping came from beneath the car's hood. The pinging became louder before Javier could get the car through the intersection and into the parking lot of a Seven-eleven.

"What's the matter with it?" Juan asked.

Javier shook his head in mute disgust, opened the car door, and walked around to the front of the hood. Juan followed. They peered in at the engine, but neither could see anything out of place. Javier got back in, started the motor, and let it idle. As long as he didn't step on the gas, it sounded all right. He got out and slammed the hood. "Let's see if we can get it home."

Within a block the pinging grew to a clatter as the car limped slowly to the house. Juan got the gate and Javier parked the car in the driveway. "Tomorrow, maybe someone at work will know what this means," Javier said after he got out. He stood a moment looking at the car before going in.

The next morning, the alarm went off at four. Javier got

up and stumbled into the bathroom. When he came out, he
shook Juan awake. "What time is it?" Juan asked squinting
through the eyelids that wouldn't quite open.

"Four. It takes longer to go on the bus," Javier answered.

They went through the routine of making breakfast, eating, and making lunch on the faith that they would eventu-
ally wake up. Ignoring the feeling that sand grated beneath
their eyelids, the slight nausea, the physical discomfort of
too little sleep took considerable effort.

It was still dark when they left the house to walk two
blocks to the eastbound thoroughfare where buses passed.
The air was muggy; moths battering themselves at a street
lamp were the only sign of life. They heard the bus's whirr
before they saw its square lighted windows. It pulled to the
curb, and the door gasped open for them. Except for the
driver, who took their money without speaking, the bus was
empty and looked dirtier for the absence of people. Sitting
on the plastic turquoise seats, they were aware of nothing
beyond the insistent rocking and the harshly lighted interior. The windows offered up their own reflections. Downtown, they got off to wait for a northbound bus. The sky had
turned a royal blue that would pale with heat; an orange
streetsweeper trundled past, brushing up the dirt and silence, putting down a snail's wet streak.

When Juan and Javier arrived at the company, it was
seven o'clock. They signed in and went out to the yard to
help load materials. As the foreman gave instructions, he
mentioned that they were starting a housing project in San
Marcos, north of San Antonio. It would be an hour's drive
over and back each day. Juan went with Ascensión, as was

his custom, and Javier rode with the foreman and his assistant. On the way over, Javier described his car's symptoms. The foreman said it sounded like a thrown rod, or about two hundred dollars in garage bills.

That evening, it was seven o'clock before they got back to the company. In the bus on the way home, Juan asked about the car. "Two hundred," he repeated after Javier and looked blank. "It's a lot?"

"Two hundred more than we have."

Juan thought about that a minute. "Then if we don't have the money, it can't be fixed."

"Not without money," Javier agreed. "It will have to wait till payday."

They rode the rest of the way in silence. It was nine-thirty by the time they got to the house. They bathed, cooked supper, and ate. When they fell into bed, it was eleven o'clock. Five hours later, the alarm went off.

The week passed as a treadmill of fatigue. Each morning, they got up at four; they never got to bed before eleven. At noon, they would eat as rapidly as possible to fall soundly asleep somewhere on a job site. They slept in the trucks on the way to work and on the way home. By Thursday, they were tired enough to sleep on the hard plastic seats the short distance in the bus going downtown. The distinction between sleeping and waking hours gradually crumbled as the week wore on.

Friday morning on the way to work Javier promised Juan they would take Sunday off. "One more day, and we sleep. Stay in bed till noon, get up to eat, then sleep the rest of the day. How does that sound?"

"What will you tell Joe?" Juan asked.

"That the car is broken. We don't have a way to come to work."

"It sounds good," Juan answered.

The next morning, however, when Juan remarked thankfully that it was the last day before they slept, Javier didn't answer. "We can sleep tomorrow?" Juan asked.

Javier looked away as if embarrassed. "Joe said he would pick us up at six-thirty."

"You said we could sleep."

"I told Joe about the car. He said he would come for us. We can sleep till five-thirty."

Sunday morning, the pickup stopped for them and they got in back with another worker. When they pulled up before a large house, the worker looked at the shingled roof and the attached garage and said the Spanish equivalent of, "That son-of-a-bitch. We'll never finish this."

They worked hard all day, Joe pushing them as they were never pushed at the company. The hurry, the tension, and the thought of how late they were going to have to work created bad feelings, which made it all that much more difficult. At sunset, when they had half the garage left to shingle, Joe set up spotlights. They finished the roof at nine-thirty, but by the time they cleaned up, loaded the truck, and delivered the other workers, it was eleven-thirty when Juan and Javier got home.

Juan got no farther than the front room, where he dropped on the bed. Javier went in the bathroom, then into the kitchen, where he looked in the refrigerator. "You want eggs?" he called. When Juan didn't answer, he walked into the front room carrying the skillet. "Eggs?" he said.

Juan stared at the pink ceiling, then shook his head.

"If you're going to work, you have to eat."

"I'm not going to work." Juan looked at Javier.

Javier met his gaze, the electric fan tapping dully in the background, then turned back to the kitchen. He put the skillet on a burner, broke in six eggs, and lanced the yolks with a fork before stirring. On another burner, he dropped a flour tortilla over the blue gas flame until he could smell it beginning to burn, then plucked it up to turn it over. He divided the eggs between two plates, poured hot sauce over them, put tortillas on the side, and took them into the front room. He put Juan's plate on the bed next to him, returned with forks, and sat down on a chair to eat. Without touching the eggs, Juan got up and went in the bathroom and started to shower. When he came back, he moved the plate of cold eggs to the kitchen table and lay down on the bed. "Tomorrow morning," he said to Javier, "don't try to make me go to work." He rolled over on his side to face the wall.

The next morning, Juan heard the alarm go off and Javier get up. Juan momentarily considered going to work, but closed his eyes and fell back to sleep. He woke again when the overhead light in the front room came on, thought there was still time to get up, but pulled the pillow over his face. He could hear Javier in the kitchen, then in the front room, and couldn't really sleep until the lights went off and the front door closed. With equal shares of relief and guilt, he curled up in the middle of the bed.

A noise in the kitchen woke Juan to the heat filling the closed house. He lay in bed listening, thinking that it was hot enough to be noon, until he heard something moving slowly through the dirty dishes on the kitchen table. Stealthily, Juan rolled over to Javier's side of the bed. He jumped up in the kitchen doorway to switch on the light, but caught only a glimpse of the rat as it slipped behind the refrigerator. Feeding roaches scattered on the table, stove, and around the sink. Juan opened the back door, then the front. Outside, he could see a wall of heat waves over the parking lot. He took his sky-blue pants from a nail in the wall and began to dress, putting on his pale-blue shirt and black boots. In the kitchen, he briefly considered the plate of eggs disintegrating in the heat before he decided to leave.

It was hot outside, but a relief from the closed house. Out of habit, Juan walked to the bus stop, then turned east and started in the direction of the tower. He could only see the revolving platform above the tall downtown buildings, but decided he would find out what it was. As he walked, he began to feel conspicuous. There was no one else on the sidewalk, and he wondered if he was doing something he shouldn't, if people could tell by looking that he was from Mexico. Javier had warned him not to go out till he knew how to behave, but Juan no longer cared about getting caught. It would be a free ride to Mexico.

Juan passed the fried-chicken franchise where he had eaten with Javier, and, noticing that a Mexican girl was working at the window, decided to go back. He pushed open the glass doors, and beyond, through the inside glass partition, he could see the gold chicken basking on warming trays. The girl, her hair dyed an unnatural cherry red, her eyes raccoonlike with rings of white makeup, came to the window to take his order. "What do you want?" she asked in English.

Juan looked at the menu on the wall behind her. He could make out the numbers and brand names of soft drinks. "*Pollo,*" he said.

"How many pieces?" she switched to Spanish.

At a small table next to the window, Juan ate the chicken out of the hot, greasy box. He went back outside, taking what was left of his Pepsi, and continued in the direction of the tower. He crossed beneath the expressway overpass and walked along the edge of small parking lots behind a series of restaurants and stores. In the next block, he noticed a sign in a restaurant window advertising in Spanish that help was wanted. He walked on, passed a cathedral, and crossed a small plaza. The tall buildings began to close in, making the car horns echo loudly and trapping the heat. Suddenly there were crowds of people on the sidewalk and the tower was out of sight. Reasoning that beyond the buildings he would find the tower again, he started in as through a chasm, then decided he should investigate the job in the restaurant first.

The man behind the cash register told Juan to talk to the manager in back and pointed a thumb over his shoulder. Crossing through the first dining room, Juan noticed a waiter setting tables and approved of the short white jacket and black bow tie he wore. Juan went through another dining room and on through swinging service doors. A Mexican woman folding red tablecloths directed him on toward the open door of a small office. When he tapped shyly on the doorframe, a woman wearing glasses looked up from the desk. "About the sign," he said.

She looked at Juan till "the sign" registered, sized him up, and took off her glasses. Middle-aged, she appeared to be the sort of woman who went to the beauty shop once a week and thought a good deal of money. "You've got a Social Security number," she said in Spanish. Juan nodded yes. "You come in every night at seven. Mop and wax the floors, clean. The dining rooms have to be spotless. Seven to seven, seven nights a week." She raised her eyebrows.

"Can I tell you tomorrow?"

She lowered her head in consent. "If no one else has taken it."

On the way out, Juan noticed the brown tile floors and saw that there were three dining rooms in all. The restaurant hadn't seemed so large until he looked at all the tables and chairs and imagined moving them to mop. Walking home, he considered the advantages of the restaurant. The work wouldn't be so heavy or hot as at the company, and it was close enough to walk. He would stay long enough to buy gifts to take home.

The house was hotter still when Juan got back. He opened the doors, took off his shirt, and turned on the fan. It was too hot to lie down on the bed, so he washed the dirty dishes and stacked them on the counter to dry. When he finished, he sat on the back step till he noticed a patch of shade beneath a dusty chinaberry tree that he judged was just right for a nap. He got a blanket, latched the front screen door, and went out back to make himself comfortable in the shade.

When Juan woke, it was late afternoon, the time when he and Javier would be getting back from the company. The thought of Javier made Juan nervous. He got up, went in the kitchen, and poured himself a glass of punch. Realizing he was hungry, he decided to go ahead and make the tortillas. He ate two with margarine, then swept the floor, made the bed, and straightened the front room. He was sitting in the dark on the front step, listening to the thud of the jukebox, when he saw Javier come walking in across the parking lot. From the way he walked and opened the gate, Juan could see how tired Javier was. Neither of them spoke. Juan stood up to let Javier pass, then followed him into the house.

Javier sat on the end of the bed, his lunch box on the floor where he dropped it. He was leaning forward, his forearms rested on his spread knees, his hands like stiff leather work gloves dangling before him. His head hung down as if he were studying the floor between his feet.

"I got a job," Juan said.

Javier cocked his head with interest but without looking up.

"At a restaurant downtown," Juan went on. "I saw the sign in the window and they said I could have the job mopping and waxing the floors. I go to work at night. Seven nights a week."

Javier's right hand gave the left hand an investigative push to make it swing like a pendulum, then plucked up a

piece of loose skin when it came to a halt. "How much do
they pay?" he asked.

"Oh." Juan realized he hadn't asked. "They didn't say."

"And overtime. Do they pay overtime?"

"I don't know."

Javier's left hand gave the right a push. When it swung to
a halt, Javier looked up at Juan. His face was exhausted except for the eyes. "You and me," he said, "what we have is
work. If we couldn't work, no one would want us." He
looked down at his hands and was silent a moment. "Work
is all we have and the only way we can lift ourselves. But
you have to pay attention. It's like a lesson, work. If you
don't pay attention, you don't learn or move ahead."

He looked up at Juan again, and saw he didn't understand, then looked down at his hands. "When I came here, I
was like you. I didn't know anything. The first day, I was
walking down the street and saw some men making a sidewalk. I asked them if there was work and they sent me to
the boss. He looked at me and said, 'Do you know how to
work?' I was scared. I had never worked here, didn't know if
I could do what he wanted, but said, 'Yes, I know how to
work.' I had to.

"So I worked hard that day. Shoveled dirt. The other men
told me not to work so hard, but I didn't mind. I was afraid
he wouldn't pay me. At the end of the day, the boss gave me
$8.00. Enough for my room and something to eat. The next
day, I learned how to mix cement. I kept working hard and
at the end of the third day he gave me $10.00. And told me
not to tell the other men. It made me happy till I heard one
of the men say he was getting $1.75 an hour. Then I knew

that the boss was cheating me. I thought I might quit, but I couldn't, and I was beginning to see how the work was done here so I kept watching, then went to the boss. When I asked for more money, he said, 'Javier, do you have the Social Security card?' I said, 'No.' I didn't know what that was. He said I couldn't work without one, but if I would stay, he would get me one. So I stayed. When the card came, he showed it to me, but said he would keep it so I wouldn't lose it. He kept it because he didn't want me to leave. But he started to pay me like the others, so I didn't complain.

"At the end of the month, I knew how sidewalks were made. The man who brought the sand in the dump truck had been watching me. He said I was a good worker and asked if I wanted to come with him. I said no, that I was learning about sidewalks, and the boss had my card. He told me the boss had no right to keep my card, that I had rights. He said he would get my card for me and would teach me how to drive the truck. So I got my card and learned how to drive, and he helped me get my driver's license. But the important thing I learned was that if I worked hard, I would have some rights and a better chance would come along."

Javier sat up on the bed and looked at Juan. "Since then, I've always learned something at work, and each job I've had has been a better job."

He stopped a minute as if he had run down, then asked Juan, "You know why I'm working for Joe on Sundays?" Juan shook his head. "Not because he pays good but because I want to see what he's doing. If he can work alone, then so can we. The hard part is getting the jobs and learning how to bid. The rest we can do. I've started buying tools. As soon as we get the car fixed and paid for, I'm going to trade it in on a pickup. Then we can look for our own jobs."

Juan looked skeptical. "You don't have papers," he objected. "Joe is legal."

Javier narrowed his eyes as if shading them from the truth of what Juan said. "It doesn't matter. People say I'm crazy, but I don't care. They told me I couldn't come here to work, but I came. They always told me what I couldn't do and it never stopped me. Five times they caught me and sent me back, and five times I've returned. Once they know me in one place on the river, I go to another place to cross. They can't keep me out."

Juan shrugged nervously and shook his hair back over his collar. Javier caught himself, exhaled a deep sigh, and continued in a calm tone of voice. "Someone from the garage is going to come tomorrow for the car. Wednesday, we get paid. We can drive to work on Thursday, and you can drive again." He looked at Juan.

"At the company, they'll take me back?" Juan asked.

"I told them you were sick."

Juan thought a moment, then shrugged.

As Javier promised, the car was repaired, they were able to drive to work, and Juan continued his lessons. Each morning they slept till five, and at night, they were in bed by ten. On Saturday, they worked for the company; on Sunday, they worked for Joe. Slowly they began to catch up on sleep, and, freed from the bus schedule, their lives began to return to normal.

The following week, the crew got an assignment in San Antonio. It meant less time on the road, more time at home. Tuesday night, Juan and Ascensión left the job site a few minutes before the others. When they got back to the company, Juan went out to the parking lot to wait in the car. As Javier was returning to English class that night, Juan didn't expect a driving lesson and got in on the passenger's side. He sat watching the other men coming out, trying to guess which car each would go to and daydreaming about what kind of car he would like to have. The parking lot emptied, shadows grew long, the flow of men dwindled and finally stopped.

Juan turned in his seat a couple of times to look toward headquarters. Javier, he imagined, was inside talking with some of the others. It was getting so late, he wondered if Javier had decided not to go to class. Perhaps he would get to drive after all, Juan was thinking, when the foreman with the fierce-looking mustache and sideburns stuck his face through the driver's window. "Hey, Julio," he said. "Immigration stopped us on the way home and got Frank. Frank asked me to give you these." He held out the car keys for Juan.

A YEAR LATER, in the summer of 1978, Javier was back in San Antonio working for the roofing company. He had, since returning from Mexico, purchased a pickup to be used for independent jobs and fathered a native-born American son.

The Border Patrol caught Juan once during the year. He stayed in his village long enough to get restless, then came back to San Antonio. In the summer of 1978, he too was working for the roofing company and, like so many people his age, was thinking that love and marriage might be the way.